GUN
SAFETY
IN THE HOME

MASSAD AYOOB

Published by

Gun Digest® Books, an imprint of F+W Media, Inc.
Krause Publications • 700 East State Street • Iola, WI 54990-0001
715-445-2214 • 888-457-2873
www.krausebooks.com

To order books or other products call toll-free 1-800-258-0929
or visit us online at www.gundigeststore.com

ISBN-13: 978-1-4402-3987-8
ISBN-10: 1-4402-3987-8

Design by Sharon Bartsch
Edited by Corrina Peterson

Printed in United States of America

CONTENTS

////////////////////////////

DEDICATION

I dedicated my first gun safety book, decades ago, to my daughters. I lovingly dedicate this one to my grandchildren. May they grow up with the same safety, responsibility, and competence as their mothers, who each won national shooting championships in their teens.

INTRODUCTION

Every reader has a right to know where the author is coming from. One of my earliest memories is shooting my older sister's Springfield Model 87 .22 rifle. My father held it balanced on his palm a bit ahead of the trigger guard while I, too short to properly shoulder it, sorta climbed over the stock to aim and fire. Dad told me I was four years old the first time we did that.

Fast forward: I started carrying a loaded, concealed handgun when I went to work in the family jewelry store at the age of 12, legal in that time and place. I started informal competition in local "turkey shoots" at about 15, and was 19 when family friend Nolan Santy introduced me to formal NRA pistol competition. By age 25 I had become a published gun writer, a police firearms instructor, and a state champion in police combat shooting. I'm 65 at this writing. You do the math; it's too depressing for me.

There have been a whole lot of bullets put safely downrange since. It has taught me a few things about safety, which are shared here. In the end, it's all about common sense.

"Use things the way they're meant to be used." We say that a lot as parents and grandparents; we need to constantly say it to ourselves. "Keep your appendages away from the working parts." We do that with table saws and lawnmowers and need to apply it to firearms, too. I've been the handgun editor for Guns magazine for thirty-some years, and a few years ago I began one column with words to the effect of, "I am holding my friend's little finger. Unfortunately, he's standing across the room." He had been working the slide of his 1911 .45 pistol from the front instead of the back when it unintentionally discharged and he wound up with nine digits on his hands instead of ten. He asked the people at the hospital to preserve the amputated finger in Formalin. It's a helluva good visual aid when he discusses firearms safety, and teaches people not to end up as he did.

Firearms, if you think about it, are power tools. They drill holes in things and chew things up. That's their purpose. The purpose of the user is, quite simply, to puncture and destroy the right things and not the wrong things.

Many experts will be resourced here. I've learned too much from too many to do an "acknowledgements" page, because I would inadvertently leave some out and hurt someone's feelings. In the end, the focus on safety should be credited to the entire firearms-owning community, the "gun culture" if you will. Contrary to pervasive media propaganda, deaths and injuries inflicted with firearms have gone down in the last several years, despite a huge increase in the number of guns owned privately in the United States.

The following is written in hope of continuing that trend.

CHAPTER ONE

CORE FIREARMS SAFETY PRINCIPLES

"The Devil loads the empty gun"

— Old Latin American saying

The firearm is defined at law as a lethal weapon. The hunter uses it as sporting equipment. The farmer uses it as a tool. The target shooter literally uses it as a remote control paper punch. And, from homeowners to police to military, many people carry them expressly because they are deadly weapons, the only effective tool that can ward off homicidal humans who have lethal capability of their own and are trying to murder the legitimate owners of those guns, or innocent victims within their mantle of protection.

We spend our lives surrounded by dangerous equipment. Automobiles. Anything electrical. Gasoline and countless other flammables and explosives, drain cleaner, powerful medications and countless other toxic substances. Power tools, of which the gun is one – in essence, an explosively operated drill that works from a distance.

We must use them all with the utmost care. We must be thoroughly familiar with their proper use. We are responsible for keeping them out of the hands of those who might do harm with them. That category includes unsupervised children, but also encompasses irresponsible or incompetent adults, and anyone who might intentionally use them to commit wrongful acts. This in turn encompasses protecting them from theft. A huge percentage of criminals who commit "gun crimes" do so with firearms stolen from the law-abiding. There are probably only two products thieves can steal from you that they can sell on the black market for more than their intrinsic value, instead of fencing them for pennies on the dollar: prescription drugs and deadly weapons.

Let's examine some well-established rules of firearms safety. The longest standing are "The Ten Commandments of Gun Safety." They have appeared in various forms over the generations. Here is a current version, from Remington Arms.

THE TEN COMMANDMENTS OF FIREARMS SAFETY
(from the Remington Arms website, www.remington.com)

- Always keep the muzzle pointed in a safe direction.
- Firearms should be unloaded when not actually in use.
- Don't rely on your gun's safety.
- Be sure of your target and what's beyond it.
- Use proper ammunition.
- If your gun fails to fire when the trigger is pulled, handle with care.
- Always wear eye and ear protection when shooting.
- Be sure the barrel is clear of obstructions before shooting.
- Don't alter or modify your gun and have it serviced regularly.
- Learn the mechanical and handling characteristics of the firearm you are using.

Now, let's look at each of those directives in more depth.

ALWAYS KEEP THE MUZZLE POINTED IN A SAFE DIRECTION

This will ideally mean that the gun is always pointed at something which can safely absorb the most powerful round that particular gun can fire. Up in the air when outdoors seems safe, but every year people are killed or injured by the foolish practice of celebratory gunfire, that is, firearms discharged upward like relatively harmless fireworks. A few years ago, a hunter emptied his muzzleloader at the end of a day afield by firing it skyward. The bullet came down a great distance away and struck in the head a teenage Amish girl in a horse-drawn buggy, killing her.

This element of gun safety is why other detectives get nervous when one investigator in the squad room is carrying his pistol in a horizontal shoulder holster: anyone standing behind him is in line with the muzzle. It is one reason why many shooters refuse to wear an appendix holster, which holds the muzzle of the gun in line with the genitalia and the femoral artery, particularly when the wearer is seated. A gun in a holster, if left alone, is most unlikely to become possessed by demons and fire by itself. However, I remember the off-duty cop in a crowded theater who said he was "adjusting" his pistol in its concealed shoulder holster when it discharged. Fortunately, nobody was hit by the bullet.

FIREARMS SHOULD BE UNLOADED WHEN NOT ACTUALLY IN USE

The gun being carried by a police officer or, for that matter, a private citizen with a carry permit, actually is in use, and so is the defensive firearm stored in a place of business or the home. That use is sentinel duty, emergency equipment ready to be immediately employed to save life.

DON'T RELY ON YOUR GUN'S SAFETY

Anything made by man can fail. I have seen semiautomatic pistols whose thumb safety was so out of adjustment that when the trigger was pulled, an observer could see the untouched safety lever appear to pull itself down from "safe" to "fire" position as the hammer fell and discharged the pistol.

This certainly should not be taken as advice to NOT use the manual safety, especially when the gun is carried loaded. We will never know how many people were saved from shooting themselves in the leg when the trigger caught a poorly designed safety strap or a coat's adjustment cord as it was being holstered, solely because an engaged manual safety kept the pistol from discharging when the trigger was "artificially pulled." We do know that there have been many, many cases where a criminal has gotten a gun away from a good guy, usually a cop, tried to shoot him with his own pistol, and failed because the criminal couldn't find the inconspicuous little safety lever that "turned the gun on." We'll never know how many hunters were saved in the woods when they were maneuvering through a thicket and a tree branch snapped inside the trigger guard, hard enough to discharge the gun, and the rifle or shotgun remained silent because the safety catch was engaged.

BE SURE OF YOUR TARGET AND WHAT'S BEYOND IT

In the south, a police officer shot at a poisonous snake in a tree. The bullet continued its flight, eventually coming down to strike a young boy far from the officer and out of his line of sight. Hunting videos exist where you can see a hunter aim at what appears to be a single antelope or hog, and fire. That animal falls, revealing an animal behind it that staggers and falls as well. Unseen by the hunter, it has been killed or wounded by a bullet passing through the intended target.

Always remember that on the range, shooting from a low position such as kneeling or prone may angle your shots upward, over the bullet-stopping backstop or berm. Always take a careful line of sight before firing. Similarly, firing at targets on the ground midway between shooter and berm can cause bullets to ricochet on an angle that may allow them to escape the range with tragic results. One reason police and responsible homeowners and concealed carriers load their defensive firearms with hollow point bullets and similar rounds designed to stay inside the body of the offender is that this target is the only backstop they have. A projectile that pierces through and through the violent attacker may kill or cripple an innocent person behind him, blocked from the shooter's view by any number of things: distance, darkness, tunnel vision, a curtain or sheetrock wall, or the imposing bulk of the offender himself.

USE PROPER AMMUNITION

This writer was on the board of directors of a good-size gun club when called to respond to the range due to a gun blow-up. A member had been sighting in his two hunting rifles, a .308 and a .270. He was using the same brand of ammo, in similar packages, for both. He became so wrapped up in his shooting that when he reloaded his .270, he accidentally plucked .308 rounds from the other box and put them into the gun. The .308 Winchester cartridge is shorter than the .270 Winchester, so the bolt action closed on the live .308 round, the bullet tip of which was barely in the .270's chamber. However, the bullet was too wide for the bore – the inside of the barrel – and when he fired, pressure spiked and the gun blew up spectacularly. His face was badly cut, and because he was wearing flimsy sunglasses instead of proper eye protection, he suffered some permanent impairment of vision.

IF YOUR GUN FAILS TO FIRE WHEN
THE TRIGGER IS PULLED, HANDLE WITH CARE

The "hangfire," in which the cartridge fires a short time after its primer has been struck by the firing pin, is mostly seen with old-fashioned black powder guns, but can occur with modern ammunition at least in theory. In training for defensive emergencies, most of us will simply eject that cartridge and chamber another.

Far more dangerous, in this writer's opinion, is the gun that goes "poof" instead of "bang," or seems to have no recoil. If that happens, STOP! It is usually a signal that a weak round, called a squib, has just been fired. These will often lodge a bullet in the barrel. If another full power round is fired behind it, the resulting pressure spike will very likely explode the gun, causing serious injury or even death. Carefully remove all other ammunition from the gun, and run a cleaning rod or something similar down the barrel to check for obstructions.

ALWAYS WEAR EYE AND EAR PROTECTION WHEN SHOOTING

This also goes for anyone else on the range, whether they're shooting or not. Hearing damage from gunfire is cumulative, and serious hearing loss often does not show up for years. Audiologists tell me it is not reversible. I strongly suggest ear plugs *and* ear muffs, particularly with high powered

Keep your firearms well maintained and in good working order. This neglected 1911 pistol has obstructions in the bore that could make it dangerous to shoot.

A damaged gun can be a dangerous gun. After it went through a house fire, gunsmiths declared this fine old Smith & Wesson .38 no longer safe to shoot.

Badly rusted, this neglected 1911 .45 magazine is no longer reliable.

rifles and loud Magnum handguns, and any other firearm with a particularly sharp, high-decibel report. Well-fitted plugs give the illusion of the same sound attenuation you get with good muffs, but audiologists tell us that much of the sound impulse which causes the high range nerve deafness we call shooter's ear comes by way of vibrations through the mastoid bone, against which plugs offer little or no protection. Muffs do shield that area. However, the stems of the safety glasses we must wear while shooting break the seal of

Clean guns are safer guns. This is the handy Otis cleaning kit – developed by a sixteen-year-old girl!

KNOW THY FIREARM WELL! These are both SIG-Sauer P-series pistols, but the one on left is single action only, shown here cocked and locked with manual safety in the "safe" position. There is no such device on the double action version at right, which has a decocking lever instead of a manual safety.

the muffs at a critical juncture, allowing noise in. The plugs are a safety net to allow for that. Hence, plugs and muffs.

I'd urge you to invest in active hearing protectors, for reasons of safety as well as performance. Amplifying low sounds but reducing loud ones, these allow you to hear range commands. One of my fellow instructors was about to give a "fire" command to a line of shooters at a police range he'd been assured had nothing to harm behind the brush of the

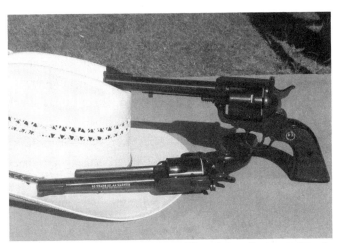

Single action revolvers like these operate differently from the more commonly seen double action designs. This is author's pair of Ruger Blackhawk .44 Magnums.

backstop, when he heard something in that brush through his enhanced muffs. He gave a cease fire command. Moments later, a mentally-challenged man wandered out of the brush where the officers had been about to unleash a fusillade that might well have killed him had the instructor not been wearing active hearing protectors.

Eye protection is critical, without it, this writer would have been totally blind before reaching voting age. One day in my early teens I was shooting a WWII surplus Czech .380 pistol. It had apparently been made late in the war with slave labor, sloppy or perhaps even sabotaged workmanship, and poor heat treating. A few shots into the shooting session, the firing pin retainer crystallized. On the next shot, the firing pin came straight back out of the gun, directly at my right eye. It would have skewered my eyeball through the pupil like a toothpick in a martini olive had it not been for my tempered eyeglasses, which were chipped and cracked by the violent impact. Not long after, I was shooting a cheap ($12.95) .22 Short revolver at a small steel bullet trap in my basement when, at the first shot – WHAM! Something struck me violently in the face, hard enough to knock my eyeglasses off. It turned out that the shoddy revolver had been assembled with the barrel screwed in off-thread, causing it to shoot far to the left. The low-powered .22 Short bullet had struck the reinforced outer edge of the bullet trap and come straight back. The left lens of my eyeglasses was cracked, but had stopped the bullet from excavating my eye socket.

Wear protective glasses while cleaning guns, too! Ace firearms instructor Bob Smith in Coeur d'Alene, Idaho, shows his students the cracked safety glasses he was wearing when he was taking apart an AK47, and one powerful spring got loose and came flying at him. The lens was ruined, but stopped the flying steel short of Bob's eye. The glasses serve other purposes in cleaning: I've been hit inadvertently in the eye with a shot of carbon tetrachloride-based gun cleaning spray, and it's a toss-up whether I'd rather do that again or take another training hit of OC pepper spray directly in the eyes.

BE SURE THE GUN BARREL IS CLEAR OF OBSTRUCTIONS BEFORE SHOOTING

See above. I miss the plugged bottoms of the police holsters I wore in the years after I first pinned on a badge, and always preferred them for outdoorsman use. The reason is that something as simple as falling on your butt in snow or mud, or squatting in a snowdrift to examine a deer track, can inadvertently immerse the handgun's muzzle in muck or snow if the holster has an open bottom. The same is true of falling forward into such substances. Soldiers have learned to put masking tape or even condoms over the muzzles of their combat rifles for just this reason.

DON'T ALTER OR MODIFY YOUR GUN, AND HAVE IT SERVICED REGULARLY

This rule bears some discussion. Most competitive shooters use guns modified for high performance, but are extremely careful to make sure they don't violate safety specs. With defensive firearms, it has become common in the legal world to falsely allege that a legitimate, deliberate self-defense shooting was actually negligent and unintended. There are several reasons for this. First, there is no such thing as a "justifiable accident." Second, in criminal court a politically-motivated prosecutor can much more easily convince the jury that a good guy got careless and made an indefensible mistake (manslaughter) than that he turned into a bad guy and killed with genuine malice (murder). Third, in a civil lawsuit, alleging that you the defendant shot his client deliberately shuts the plaintiff's lawyer out of the deep pockets of your insurance company, which only covers for negligence and is generally expressly exempt from having to pay for your having deliberately harmed that lawyer's client, a willful tort.

When opposing counsel is going in that direction and trying to show you to be reckless and negligent, you DON'T want to give him a weapon as powerful as "Ladies and gentlemen of the jury, this defendant DEACTIVATES THE SAFETY DEVICES ON LETHAL WEAPONS!!"

Similarly, "hair triggers" have long been associated with

unintended discharges, and indeed have become a byword in the common parlance for people who "go off" when they shouldn't. A trigger pull of less weight than the manufacturer's specification for duty use is very deep quicksand in court. I've warned for years that the very light trigger pull is a two-edged sword. "The good news is, it's easy to shoot. The bad news is, it's easy to shoot."

LEARN THE MECHANICAL AND HANDLING CHARACTERISTICS OF THE FIREARM YOU ARE USING

Over the years, one problem we've seen is that novices – or people distracted, fatigued, confused, or terrified – perform functions out of sequence. The classic example with a firearm is that instead of unloading by removing the magazine and then clearing the firing chamber, they do that backwards. They clear the chamber, ejecting the round therein, and don't realize that they have just chambered another live round with the same action. They then remove the magazine and consider the gun empty, when in fact there's a live torpedo in the launch tube and when the trigger is pulled, the gun will fire. This has been known to end tragically.

It's important to know whether or not your gun is drop-safe, that is, whether it is capable of firing due to an inertia discharge if it is dropped on a hard surface, struck sharply, or subjected to the violent G-forces of a car crash. When in doubt, call the manufacturer, request the service department, and ask this specific question.

Long after the "Ten Commandments of Firearms Safety" became the standard, a WWII combat vet and master firearms instructor came along with something simplified, and geared specifically for defensive firearms. He was Lt. Col. Jeff Cooper, USMC (ret.), and his Four Rules have become a generic standard among modern gun people.

JEFF COOPER'S FOUR RULES

Col. Cooper's Four Rules were, in essence:

• Every gun is always loaded.

• Never allow the muzzle to point at anything you are not prepared to see destroyed.

• Keep your finger out of the trigger guard until your sights are on target.

• Always be certain of your target and what is behind it.

Cooper had brilliantly simplified the Ten Commandments for what another gun expert, Peter Kokalis, defined as Armed Professionals. It was understood they'd have guns they knew and the right ammunition. Even so, there are semanticists in

COOPER'S RULE #1:
All guns are always loaded – or treated as carefully as if they were.

COOPER'S RULE #2: Never point the gun at anything you are not prepared to destroy. Here, pistol champ Gail Pepin, shooting right to left, strafes down a row of steel plates with her 9mm Glock.

COOPER'S RULE #3: Keep finger out of trigger guard until you are actually shooting, as demonstrated here.

every discipline, and the world of the gun is no exception. Let's take a quick, interpretive look at the Four Rules.

EVERY GUN IS ALWAYS LOADED

I don't believe the Colonel meant this literally. Would you walk into a gun show or even a gun shop if every firearm on display for handling were loaded? I've visited the Colonel at his famous home, The Sconce, on the grounds of the Gunsite Training Center he created. Adorning the walls of his den were firearms he had made famous: his personal Bren Ten; the 8 3/8-inch barrel Smith & Wesson .44 Magnum he preferred for hunting; and the Browning Hi-Power in caliber .40 G&A that he had created with Whit Collins for the eponymous Guns & Ammo magazine, the journal in which he first earned fame. None of those guns were loaded when I saw them and examined them at his invitation. I believe what he was saying was simply, "Treat every gun as if it is loaded." It is widely known that unloaded guns cause the most tragedies, i.e., that foolish people do stupid things with them when they think they're incapable of harm.

NEVER POINT YOUR GUN AT ANYTHING YOU ARE NOT PREPARED TO DESTROY

In the world of firearms safety, wiser words were never spoken. This is why there should always be a safe backstop behind the aiming point even during dry fire. You always want every possible safety net. I explain to my students, "Look, I don't know you people yet, so until I do, don't point your guns at anything *I'm* not prepared to see destroyed, and we'll get along fine."

KEEP YOUR FINGER OUT OF THE TRIGGER GUARD
UNTIL YOUR SIGHTS ARE ON TARGET

Often stated as "on target, on trigger; off target, off trigger," I respectfully suggest that this rule should go farther. It's fine for the shooting range, but in a danger situation where violent criminal suspects may be taken at gunpoint, at that moment the sights ARE on target and this interpretation of the rule would then put the finger on the trigger. Now, the person holding the gun is just one mishap away from accidentally killing a suspect who has surrendered to him and offered no harm.

Dr. Roger Enoka is the physiologist who has done the most comprehensive and ground-breaking work on physiology applied to accidental firearms discharges. He notes that several things may cause spasmodic, unintended discharges if the finger is on the trigger. These include startle response, whether the stimulus is a loud sound or an unexpected touch; interlimb response (in which the gun hand's fingers all tighten when the other hand closes, as when applying handcuffs); and postural disturbance, because when we lose our balance we instinctively clutch for something to hold us upright.

With that in mind, I would suggest this rule, one that I enforce at my own school: THE FINGER WILL ONLY BE INSIDE THE TRIGGER GUARD WHEN WE ARE IN THE VERY ACT OF INTENTIONALLY FIRING THE GUN!

Not "when we're ready to shoot." Hell, we should be ready to shoot when we put the gun on. Not "when we're on target." History shows that, for every time the trigger has to be pulled, cop and citizen alike will take many criminals at gunpoint and end matters with that act alone.

COOPER'S RULE # 4: Always be certain of your target and what is behind it.

ALWAYS BE CERTAIN OF YOUR TARGET
AND WHAT IS BEHIND IT

I can't add much to that which hasn't been said elsewhere here.

It is sad that so many people use Col. Cooper's Four Rules without paying proper homage and crediting where they came from. That is a shame, because his work has undoubtedly saved more lives and more suffering than any of us will ever know.

Revolvers are easier to "show clear" than autoloaders, as seen here with a Taurus Ultra-Lite .22 Magnum.

Keep the finger outside the trigger guard until you are in the very act of intentionally discharging the firearm, author counsels. Pistol is a 1911 .45 auto.

Ray Millican, retired Army Special Forces Sergeant-Major, demonstrates safe unloading of semiautomatic pistol. First, his Smith & Wesson Military & Police Compact is pointed in a safe direction . . .

. . then, with fingers clear of trigger guard, he removes the magazine first . . .

. . . and puts it away before proceeding further. This is important because it frees up his support hand to perform support functions with maximum strength and dexterity, and prevents unsafe "juggling" of magazine and pistol . . .

CHAPTER ONE: Core Firearms Safety Principles **29**

. . . now, with dominant hand maintaining control and keeping muzzle safely downrange, support hand retracts slide, ejecting cartridge from chamber to ground. Next . . .

... is CHECKING BY FEEL. Dominant hand holds pistol steady while little finger of support hand (for most people, the narrowest of the ten digits) probes the magazine well to make sure the mag is out . . .

. . . and then the chamber to make sure it's empty. Making this a habit will fail-safe you if you have to check the gun in the dark. It should aways be used when checking for unloaded status, and not just when removing cartridges.

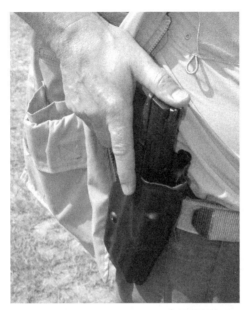

Retired Special Forces Sergeant-Major Ray Millican demonstrates safe holstering. Thumb "rides" the slide, keeping it forward in battery, and straight index finger "points" S&W M&P safely into Safariland holster. On hammer-fired gun, thumb holds double action hammer down or single action hammer back, another safety net.

Any firearm can jam, and it's important to know how to clear it.

AUTHOR'S SAFETY RULES

When you teach the gun, you're responsible for the safety of the students, the training staff, and of course, yourself. Here are the rules I've gone by for a very long time:

MASSAD AYOOB GROUP (MAG) SAFETY RULES: LIVE FIRE

First, the four core safety rules originally promulgated by Col. Jeff Cooper:

A: Treat every firearm as if it is fully loaded and ready to discharge.

Parade rest in action on the firing line. By simply leaning back at the hips, each shooter can see that every other is no longer holding a firearm.

B: Never point a firearm at anything you are not prepared to destroy.

C: Do not allow your trigger finger to be inside the trigger guard unless and until you are in the very act of intentionally firing the weapon.

D: Always be certain of your target and what is behind it.

When on a "cold range," gun will be unloaded at all times until you are instructed to load by instructor or range officer.

When manipulating the slide of a semiautomatic pistol, keep the muzzle downrange in a safe direction and do not

This new shooter has been given 55-gallon drum to serve as table. Having place to set gun reduces fatigue, prevents straying muzzles. Her Smith & Wesson revolver is safely open and can be readily seen to be unloaded.

allow hand, forearm, or other body parts to come in line with the muzzle. Retract the slide by grasping it at the rear, NOT from the front.

When unloading a semiautomatic pistol, remove magazine first and put it somewhere – pocket, pouch, or waistband – so support hand can be dedicated to slide manipulation, and primary hand can be dedicated to holding the gun in a safe direction, without either hand having to "juggle" the magazine.

When clearing the chamber of a semiautomatic pistol, allow the cartridge to fall to the ground and retrieve it later. Do NOT eject a live cartridge into the palm, or attempt to catch it in mid-air.

If you drop a gun, let it fall. Grabbing at a falling gun

The gentle hand of a coach is seen behind the shoulder of this new young shooter, to prevent too much muzzle rise as his Taurus 9mm recoils.

At Live Oak Police Department Teen Academy range day, Chief Buddy Williams explains S&W M&P15 .22 rifle and its magazine to students.

Range officer has safely stepped slightly forward of the firing line to visually confirm that all pistols have been gently, safely grounded as teens fill magazines preparatory to shooting.

A strong stance that controls recoil helps new shooters get over fear of recoil. This young lady starts leaning back, exacerbating muzzle jump . . .

. . . but as soon as coach gets her to put body weight forward, she achieves much more confidence and control with 9mm Ruger pistol.

It's a good idea to have one coach/safety officer for every one or two new shooters.

Author demonstrates double action semiautomatic pistol to a group of teen academy students.

Demonstration is important to learning safety as well as marksmanship.

Under rigid police supervision, these teens learn to shoot AR15 rifles in .22 caliber.

often results in unintentional pressure applied to the trigger, causing discharge in an uncontrollable direction.

When holstering any handgun, keep the trigger finger STRAIGHT outside the trigger guard, and use the thumb to safely keep single action auto's hammer from falling forward, or double action auto's hammer from rising and falling.

If your firearm malfunctions and you don't know how to clear it, keep it pointed downrange with the dominant hand and raise your support hand, which will summon a staff member to assist you.

Weapons are not to be handled after consumption of alcohol.

Advise staff (discreetly if you like) of any medical conditions, medications, etc. that may affect you while you are with us. If you are stricken, we need to know where your insulin/digitalis/etc. is.

IF YOUR MUZZLE CROSSES ANYONE INCLUDING YOURSELF – WHETHER OR NOT THE GUN IS LOADED – IT IS A SAFETY VIOLATION. THE MAG STAFF AND HOSTS RESERVE THE RIGHT TO REMOVE ANY SHOOTER FROM THE FIRING LINE FOR A SINGLE SAFETY VIOLATION, AND FOR THE REMAINDER OF THE DAY, THE STUDENT MAY OBSERVE BUT NO LONGER PARTICIPATE. HE OR SHE WILL RETURN TO THE LINE UNDER PROBATION (AND PARTICULAR SCRUTINY) THE FOLLOWING DAY. A SECOND SAFETY VIOLATION WILL RESULT IN THE STUDENT BEING IMMEDIATELY EXPELLED FROM THE PROGRAM, WITHOUT REFUND.

MASSAD AYOOB GROUP SAFETY RULES: DRY FIRE

Like virtually every training school, MAG recommends dry-fire practice to maintain manipulation skills. However, we have seen over the years that many unintended discharges occur in dry-fire, perhaps because "the empty gun" lulls the practitioner into complacency.

Follow the MAG live fire safety rules. These include, but are not limited to: treat every weapon as if it is loaded; never point it at anything you are not prepared to see destroyed; do not place your finger in the trigger guard until you are in the very act of intentionally pulling that trigger; and always be certain of your target and what is behind it.

Always check by sight and feel to confirm that the gun is in fact unloaded. THERE SHOULD BE NO LIVE AMMUNI-TION IN THE SAME ROOM WHERE YOU ARE PRACTIC-ING DRY-FIRING.

Always aim the gun at something that can safely absorb the most powerful round that particular gun can fire÷because one day, it may indeed fire that round unexpectedly. Thickly packed bookshelves with no airspace, or cartons packed with books or magazines, serve nicely as dry fire backstops. So does body armor set against a wall, and the dedicated Safe Direction™ dry-fire backstop.

Never practice trigger-pulling and reloading in the same session. It is a good idea to not even practice them on the same day.

When practicing reloading, disable the gun. A field-stripped auto pistol with only frame, slide stop, and magazine(s) suffices for practice, and guarantees no shot can be fired. With a revolver, wrap a handkerchief or rag through the topstrap of the frame so the cylinder cannot be closed into firing battery. Opening and closing the cylinder is easy: getting the cartridges into the chambers is the hard part you want to work on.

When using dummy ammunition, take great pains to be sure that live ammo has not migrated into the "dummy cartridge" supply, and vice versa.

After a dry-fire session, do not reload and holster for street carry. Give mind and body time to absorb the fact that "draw gun, pull trigger" practice is OVER.

GUN-SPECIFIC SAFETY RULES

When I say gun-specific, I mean things specific to one or another type of firearm that go beyond general gun safety rules. Let's look at shotguns, rifles, and handguns.

SHOTGUNS

The shotgun is a particularly unforgiving weapon when its output strikes a human at close range. Treat it with great respect.

Ever since my young days at trap ranges, I've been horrified to see shotgunners "rest" their weapons with the muzzles on the top of their feet. Yes, the guns are unloaded and the actions are open, but it's still a grotesque violation of a prime directive, to wit, "Don't let the muzzle point at anything you are not prepared to destroy."

One thing to be careful with when working with these "scatterguns," is that a 20-gauge shotgun shell is so dimensioned that if it is inadvertently chambered in a 12 gauge barrel, it can slide down the inside of the barrel out of sight. As the barrel constricts, the rim of the shell comes to a stop. It appears to the shooter that the chamber is empty. Then, the

The Safe Direction line of products is very handy. Here Ayoob tests the "gun bag" version . . .

... and finds that projectile from Glock 27 has been stopped easily inside the device ...

. . . which captured this 165 grain .40 caliber Gold Dot bullet rated for a nominal 1140 feet per second.

time comes when a 12-gauge shell is loaded into the chamber and, eventually, fired.

Of course, the bore is blocked by the live 20-gauge shell that has been lying in wait. That obstruction by itself will constitute a pressure spike sufficient to blow up the gun. But, remember, that obstruction is a live shell full of gun powder of its own, and it has come to rest in a narrower part of the barrel which is not constructed to take the pressure of initial discharge. The combination blows up the gun, exploding the barrel at a point where the shooter's support hand is likely to be grasping the forend. The oral history of firearms safety is replete with amputated fingers and mangled or avulsed hands resulting from this kind of safety error.

Remember that most shotguns do not have internal firing pin safeties. Their manual safety devices tend to lock the

Break-open shotguns are the easiest to load, unload, and check. This is a New England Firearms .410 single-shot.

trigger mechanisms, not the firing pins. This means that if the guns are struck hard enough on either end, an "inertia firing event" can occur when the firing pin is thrown forward of its own weight, striking the shell's primer hard enough to discharge the shell in the chamber ahead of it. The result is, BANG!

This is why, across the generations of law enforcement, police shotguns have been kept "cruiser ready," which means that the tubular magazine is loaded but the firing chamber is empty. If the shotgun was stored transversely along the front seat with a shell in the chamber, and the cruiser was T-boned or spun out and hit a tree sideways, the forces could slam the firing pin forward inside its channel without the trigger even being involved, and with a round in the chamber – BANG. If the gun was racked upright in the popular dashboard rack with a shell in the chamber, and in the course of a high speed pursuit the vehicle went over a curbing or the edge of a ditch and became airborne, when it came back down and hit, those forces would bounce the firing pin upward inside that vertical shotgun and – BANG. If the shotgun was stored in the trunk of the cruiser, perhaps with its muzzle oriented toward driver or passenger, and the police vehicle was rear-ended hard – BANG.

Know thy shotgun. The break-open, breech-loading shotgun typified by the ancient double barrel design is probably the easiest and the safest to clear. Press the release lever and "break" the gun open. The shells are right there, visible and palpable: the simplest of all administrative checking, loading, or unloading.

Slide actions and semiautomatics can be more complicated, particularly once a round has been chambered. This writer learned decades ago that no one exact protocol works on every shotgun. In both the law enforcement and the self-defense markets, the two dominant brands of slide-action shotguns have for decades been the Remington Model 870 and the Mossberg Models 500 and 590. Due to their design features, they unload differently.

With a fully loaded Remington, the protocol this writer teaches is to put the muzzle in a safe direction and, with the trigger-blocking manual safety button at the rear of the trigger guard "on safe," press the slide release at the front of the trigger guard and slowly retract the slide. The chambered

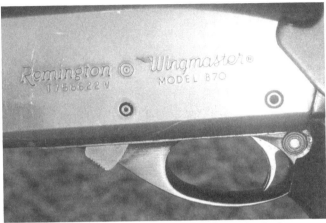

Author suggests unloading Remington 870 pump shotgun by clearing chamber and shell lifter first, then removing shells from magazine. . .

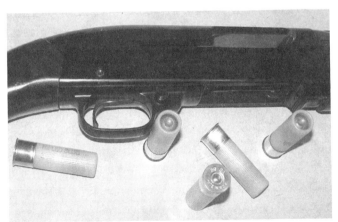

. . .but with this Mossberg 500 pump shotgun finds it more fumble-free and therefore safer to remove shells from magazine first, then clear shell from chamber. Note yellow shells for this 20-gauge, color coded to prevent dangerous mix-up with 12-gauge shells.

shell will eject; catch it in your hand or let it go to the ground to be retrieved later. The next shell in line will be sitting on the shell lift, ready to be carried into the firing chamber by the next forward stroke on the slide. Instead, roll the gun onto its ejection port side and let that shell roll out of the port. Leaving the slide to the rear, which keeps the bolt back and the ejection port open, reach in through the loading port and press the shell release at the rear of the magazine tube. This will allow the shells to pop out under spring pressure, and into your hand. Repeat until the gun is completely unloaded, its action open, and check by sight and feel to make sure.

With a fully loaded Mossberg slide action shotgun, unloading works better when the procedure is reversed. Make sure the top tang thumb safety is to the rear, "on safe." Then, we'll unload the magazine before we clear the chamber. If we try to unload it the same way as the Remington, the shell lifting mechanism will get in the way of the operator's fingers. So, on the Mossberg, we'll keep the muzzle in a safe direction as we unload every shell from the magazine, one by one just as with the Remington. Then, we'll press upward on the slide release lever at the rear of the trigger guard and slowly bring the slide back, until the "shell up the spout" comes out of the chamber through the ejection port.

The Ithaca Model 37 shotgun, once popular with police and always popular among the general public, is also best cleared magazine first, then chamber. As noted previously, know thy shotgun. Remember that most iterations of the Ithaca 37 will fire spontaneously if the slide is closed with a live shell in the chamber if the shooter's finger is holding the trigger back. The same is true of some old Winchesters, such as the Model 12 and the Model 1897.

RIFLES

Any rifle with a box magazine is best unloaded by removing the magazine (and putting the magazine in a pocket or elsewhere, so that hand is unencumbered for further manipulation of the firearm, which may still have a loaded chamber). Now, the bolt is carefully retracted to extract the chambered cartridge, which is then cleared from the rifle.

When checking by feel, IF THE RIFLE HAS BEEN RECENTLY FIRED, DO NOT insert a finger into the chamber to check by feel. High-powered rifles operate at very high pressure and can leave the firing chamber hot enough to burn human flesh. This is also true of fully automatic weapons, even submachine guns chambered for relatively low-pressure pistol cartridges.

Remember that the vast majority of rifles, irrespective of action type, do not have internal firing pin stop mechanisms that would render them drop safe. If you have ever cleared a live cartridge out of the chamber of an AR15, M16, or M4 rifle, you have probably noticed a tiny dimple on the primer that wasn't there before. It's the result of the firing pin bouncing forward in its channel when the bolt was closed to chamber that round. It hasn't hit the primer hard enough to set it off and discharge the round, but that could change with a sufficiently violent impact. If the same rifle was inside a police car (or your car) and then subjected to the tremendous inertial forces of a collision as mentioned above in the shotgun discussion, such a rifle could discharge through inertia fire without the trigger being touched.

This is why cops don't keep their patrol rifles in their vehicles with rounds chambered; they are kept "cruiser ready" like shotguns, with chamber empty and full magazine locked

Locked open on empty magazine, this Springfield M1A rifle can be safely chamber-checked with finger if the gun is cold, but if recently fired, DON'T. High-power .308 Winchester/7.62mm NATO ammo will make chamber area hot enough to burn finger.

in place. In the same vein, most military forces of the world leave their chambers empty, with the warfighters instructed to only put a round in the chamber when contact with the enemy is reasonably believed to be imminent or at least likely.

Likewise, smart outfitters and hunting guides have long advised their clients to leave their hunting rifles chamber-empty when on horseback, and urged them to chamber a round only when game was sighted. The reason is that most hunting rifles, including most lever action and bolt action arms, don't have secured firing pins either. Should the hunter drop the rifle from horseback, the gun may fall far enough that landing on the muzzle or the butt will impart sufficient force to create a firing pin inertia discharge. Even if the rifle is secured in a saddle scabbard, if the horse should fall the guide doesn't want the rifle in the scabbard to discharge.

While we're on that topic, we should address the fact that a bolt action rifle can be "un-cocked" or "de-cocked" safely by holding the bolt handle up, holding the trigger back, and then slowly closing the bolt handle downward into its locked position. Doing this with a round in the chamber was quite common among both professional hunters and their clients back in the days when this writer went on safaris on the African Continent.

That said, I can't endorse the practice with a round in the chamber. Many of those African veterans considered it safe; the hunter would quietly raise and then lower the bolt handle to cock the gun for the already-chambered round. Gunsmiths have assured me that in the un-cocked mode, the rifle's striker (firing pin) can still be subject to inertia fire. Better to follow the model of the American West: chamber empty until target sighted.

As noted in the classic Ten Commandments of Firearms Safety, a manual safety is not the be all and end all of firearms accident prevention. This AR15 is "on safe."

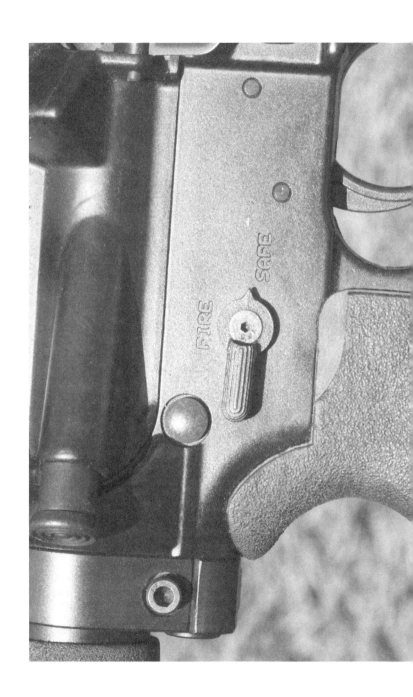

HANDGUNS

Being shorter than rifles or shotguns, handguns can more easily be pointed in improper directions. They are normally carried on the body for longer periods of time, creating greater exposure to potential mishaps.

A significant percentage of handgun accidents come during holstering and drawing the gun from the holster. In the old days, most holsters exposed the trigger guard, and the pattern of accident was that the finger would get on the trigger too early, something would snag the gun during the draw, the gun and its trigger would stop but the hand and its finger would keep moving and there would be an unexpected BANG.

In hopes of curing this, the holster industry began covering the trigger guards. This did indeed go far to preventing that type of accident. Unfortunately, in the end, it also had the effect of redistributing the pattern of unintended discharge. Now, the accidents happened during the holstering process, not during the draw. The shooter would leave the finger on the trigger, the finger would hit the edge of the holster and stop, the gun and trigger would keep going and, once again, there would be the BANG.

Ergo, as noted earlier, the rationale for the holstering process I pioneered even before establishing Lethal Force Institute in 1981. Trigger finger STRAIGHT, which everyone else was already recommending anyway, and ALSO thumb on hammer area. This held the double action gun's hammer down, so it couldn't rise or fall without the thumb feeling it in time to stop an unintended discharge. It held the cocked and locked single action auto pistol's hammer back, so if something tripped the trigger, the thumb could catch it and

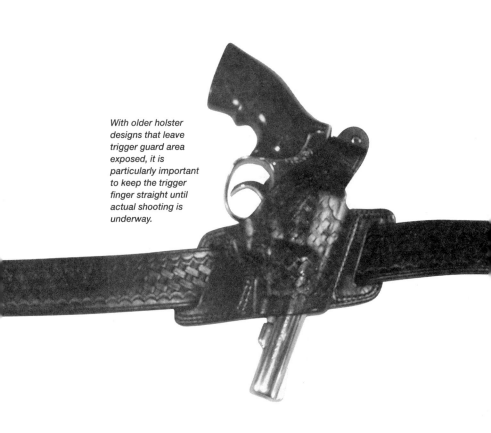

With older holster designs that leave trigger guard area exposed, it is particularly important to keep the trigger finger straight until actual shooting is underway.

block its fall. This also took the web of the hand off any existing grip safety, activating that part's safety function, yet another layer of safety.

With a striker-fired pistol that has no hammer per se, the thumb on the back still serves good purposes. It makes the shooter a better role model for others whose guns WILL be safer when holstered this way. It keeps his own gun's slide in battery; a striker-fired gun's slide comes back more easily than one whose slide is held forward by a mainspring-loaded hammer. This means that in a new or too-tight holster, the

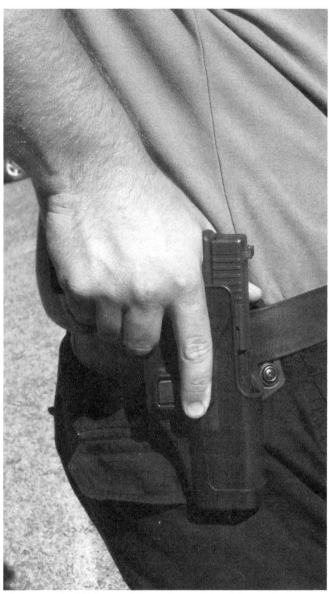

With the popular SERPA and similar holsters, author counsels pressing release paddle with fingerPRINT, not fingerTIP!

With modern holster designs that cover trigger guard, it is imperative to keep fingers (and everything else) from getting caught between trigger and holster mouth when inserting.

slide can be pushed out of battery during the insertion process, rendering the gun unshootable, as there is no guarantee that the tight holster will pull the slide back INTO battery during the draw. This holstering method guarantees that every auto pistol will be ready to shoot and defend its owner's life when it comes out of the scabbard on the shortest possible notice.

One popular holster style today, pioneered and typified by the Blackhawk SERPA, holds the gun secure with a lock

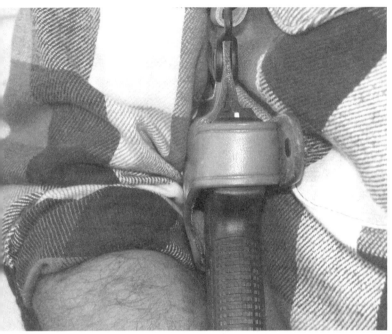

Although this Kahr pistol is perfectly safe encompassed in this left-handed shoulder holster, its muzzle points to the rear, which will alarm some people who see it.

released by pressing inward on a paddle or button with the trigger finger. It is our nature to press buttons with the tip of our finger. This points the finger inward as the gun clears the holster, and allows the fingertip to slide in, putting the index finger on the trigger prematurely. Accidental discharges resulting from this are not, in my opinion, a fault of the holster, but of the user. The paddle or button needs to be depressed with the flat part of the distal phalange of the trigger finger. The easy way to remember it is this: FINGERPRINT, NOT FINGERTIP!

Holstering protocols are covered more thoroughly in Gun

Digest Book of Concealed Carry than what I'm allowed space for here. A brief recap, however:

With a hip holster, click your heels together like a German soldier when you're holstering and tilt your upper body away from the holster: that points the muzzle farther away from your lower limbs. (Credit: master instructor David Maglio.) With an appendix holster, lean back at the hips; this puts the muzzle more out in front of you and away from the genital and femoral artery areas. (Credit: master instructor Phil Wong.) With a horizontal or vertical upside-down shoulder holster, keep the muzzle in a safe direction and turn your body to bring the holster to the gun, keeping the arm on that side raised and clear of the muzzle as the gun goes into the holster.

CHAPTER TWO

FIREARMS STORAGE IN THE HOME

A top-quality gun safe like this one is a valuable component of safe firearms storage.

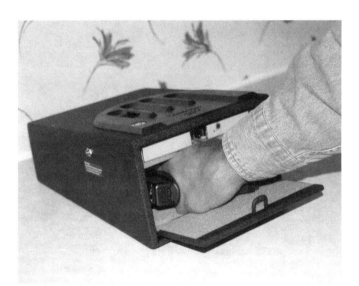

Biometric quick-access gun safe has opened immediately for THIS user, but author has found some people who just aren't compatible with biometrics.

Safe home firearms storage breaks down into two categories: simple storage and defensive-ready storage.

SIMPLE STORAGE

Simple storage is what we do with the target shooter's pistol, the outdoorsman's revolver, the hunter's rifle or shotgun. It is stored under lock and key, the key in question being available only to one or more people who have been pre-identified as logical, sound-minded individuals. Ammunition is stored in a separate location, ideally also under lock and key. For the hobbyist who has no intention of ever reaching for the gun in defense of self or others during a life-threatening emergency, Simple Storage makes sense.

This quick access safe from Gun Vault is designed to guide fingers into position for push-button combination release in the dark. Notice the key lock over-ride, important in case batteries fail. Obviously, key should not be left in lock with loaded gun inside and unattended.

A good quality safe is the best bet for this type of storage. Speed of access will not be an issue. It accomplishes a cornerstone objective: keeping the gun(s) out of the hands of those who should not have access to firearms. This includes

Author demonstrates quick release of loaded pistol inside Gun Vault.

irresponsible youngsters, equally irresponsible adults, and assorted burglars and other evildoers who might break into your home with hostile intent.

DEFENSIVE-READY STORAGE

Defensive-ready storage puts a loaded gun quickly into the hand of the person defending self and loved ones against a home invasion. Quick access to authorized hands now becomes a cornerstone priority. A gun unloaded in one locked location and ammunition locked in another location is a fine plan for simple storage, but it's simply impossible to bring the two together in time to interdict a fast-breaking home invasion. We can't alter the time/space continuum with wishful thinking.

To keep the gun securely locked yet readily accessible requires a quick-release gun safe. There are several on the market. Some use biometrics. At this writing, you'll have to test them to see if they work for you. The history of biometrics so far is that some people's hands are simply incompatible with the technology. For me, the test unit worked pretty well. For my significant other, it often failed. Conclusion: for us, at this level of its development, the technology just wasn't going to work.

Even if it had worked as well for her as for me under perfect test conditions, I still would have been leery of it. When it has to recognize your fingerprints, what's the effect of a Band-Aid on your finger that obscures your fingerprint? Or blood from a struggle after you broke free from the assailant and ran for the gun? Or dirt in the whorls of your fingerprints if you were in the garden when you heard the screaming child being attacked by a vicious dog?

In my book The Truth About Self-Protection (Police Bookshelf, PO Box 122, Concord, NH 03302), I talked about tests I did more than thirty years ago. We simply timed how long it would take for me, in the intruder role, to get to the farthest room in the house once I had breached the front door. We then timed how long it would take the homeowner to go from various rooms to where the gun was, and get it out of the storage container. The results, when correlated, were not encouraging.

What was ALWAYS the fastest for the homeowner – the ultimate, most efficient method of Defensive-Ready Storage – was for the householder to already be carrying a loaded handgun on their person.

This does not mean that the homeowner has to strap on

a Buscadero cowboy belt and a big six-shooter or two every moment they are at home. It can be something as simple as a small handgun carried concealed in the pants pocket or in an ankle holster, or a larger gun holstered inside the waistband under an un-tucked shirt. It won't frighten the postman or the UPS man or the kid selling Girl Scout Cookies who comes unexpectedly to the front door, but is immediately accessible the moment someone kicks in your door. Imagine the horror of suddenly finding a homicidal intruder already in your house after he has surreptitiously gained entry, and having to cross his path to get to your firearm.

The choice is yours. So is the responsibility for your safety and that of your family. Looking back over atrocities ranging from the massacre of the Clutter family in Kansas documented in Truman Capote's best-selling book In Cold Blood to the much more recent slaughter of the Petit family in Cheshire, Connecticut, there would have been no time for any of the victims to run to a gun safe. But, reconstruction shows that, if any of the adults present had been carrying concealed weapons, they would have had ample opportunity to turn the tables and save their own lives, and the lives of their children, from the monsters who murdered them.

"SMART GUNS"

There has been much talk of "smart guns," which only fire in the hands of their legitimate users and forbid unauthorized hands from unleashing their firepower. It's a great idea, but for the most part, it's a classic example of magical thinking. The reason is that it is what engineers call vaporware: it exists in theory, but has not been proven in the real world, with one notable exception.

Smart guns that recognize fingerprints biometrically? We've had the discussion already. Biometrics remains far from 100% for emergency life-saving equipment such as defensive firearms. Radio signals from a transmitter worn on the designated user's body? Totally unproven as yet.

The one smart gun that actually works has been with us since the mid-1970s, the Magna-Trigger device invented by the late Joe Smith and now available through Rick Devoid at Tarnhelm (www.tarnhelm.com). This is a modification of a medium-size (K-frame) or larger Smith & Wesson revolver which allows it to only be fired in the hand of a designated user wearing a special magnetic ring on the middle finger. This writer thought it was BS in the late 1970s and sacrificed a Smith & Wesson Model 66 .357 revolver to prove it. However, torture testing proved the device to work remarkably well. From the time my oldest child was three years old, that was the gun I kept at bedside fully loaded. Now that I have grandchildren, it's on standby if they come to visit.

Despite great efforts to do so, the concept has never been effectively adapted to the semiautomatic pistols police were switching to from revolvers when the Magna-Trigger came out. That's why it never became widely popular. However, it's still available, and an excellent answer to the question, "How do I keep a defense gun loaded and ready to quickly grab, without worrying about the kids getting hold of it or the bad guys taking it away from me and shooting me with it?"

CHAPTER THREE

CHILDREN AND GUNS

From electrical outlets to power saws to automobiles to household poisons to, yes, guns, there are things in American households that can hurt or kill our children. Those things must be kept from their hands until they have matured to a level of responsibility that allows them access.

A mantra of those who would ban firearms has long been, "Think of the children!" They will find a case where a child got hold of a loaded gun that was left carelessly accessible to them, with tragedy resulting, and play it up – ignoring the fact that today's kids are far more likely to drown in a family swimming pool or even a bathtub than to be killed in a firearms accident. They will also ignore the fact that accidental firearms deaths have long trended downward despite demonstrable, empirical proof that there are far more guns in American homes now than ever before.

Back in the 1980s, I wrote a short book called Gunproof Your Children. It's still in print, available from Police Bookshelf, PO Box 122, Concord, NH 03302. I called it that because, then and now, my conclusion has always been that you can't childproof your guns, so you have to gunproof your children.

The theory of hiding guns from the kids is a loser's game. Do we seriously think we are the first generation of parents to outsmart our children? Was there anything your parents could hide from you where you couldn't find it if left to your own devices?

You can secure your guns in gun safes to which only you have the combination, but you can't successfully hide them. Not from your children, and not from a burglar with unlimited time in your home. There are gun-hiding clocks and wall-hangings and such, but give unauthorized hands time enough, and they will find them. Books hollowed out to hold small handguns have been with us since the nineteenth century at least. Trouble is, that fourteen-year-old nephew you're taking care of may decide to read that book when you're not looking, and burglars know that people hide greenbacks inside the pages of ordinary books, and are known to rifle through them looking for cash.

What this writer found decades ago was that when the kids are not yet responsible, you keep the guns secure from them, where you and other responsible adults can access them and the children simply can't. It becomes clear as soon as you look at it with a practical and unbiased eye that if the gun is kept on your person, it is at once instantly accessible to you but inaccessible to unauthorized hands.

Child psychologists tell us that children crave two things

Patent Pending

Hiding guns in hollowed out books is an ancient trick, but may not fool a burglar left alone in your home.

they don't yet have: power and responsibility. Both are absolutely embodied in the gun. Look at how many heroes and power figures in the entertainment media carry and wield them. This makes guns magnets to the hands of children.

My work required me to have firearms not only in the home, but – due to death threats that stemmed from my work, and the fact that I was almost always on call for the police department I was sworn to serve – at least one or more of those guns had to be always loaded and ready. The route I took was to educate my kids in firearms. When each was five years old, I started them helping me to clean my guns. It de-mystified them, and it also de-glamorized them. ("Eew! Yuck! Gross! They're oily and dirty!") One benefit was that if one of my kids was at some other kid's house and that little brat took their daddy's gun out of the nightstand drawer, my kid knew how to unload and neutralize it – how to "de-fang the snake." Both my kids started shooting at age six, and won national champion shooting titles in their teens. Each is now a gun-owning parent of a next generation of kids who won't have tragic accidents with firearms.

One of the most successful firearms safety efforts in history is the National Rifle Association's Eddie Eagle Program. The cartoon bird tells children who come in proximity to a firearm: "STOP! DON'T TOUCH! LEAVE THE AREA! TELL AN ADULT!"

Let's break that down piece by piece, as we did with other safety rule sets earlier.

Stop! A "real gun" is an exciting thing. The very sight of it may impel a child forward to examine and handle. The initial "Stop!" phase buys time to consider the risks.

Don't touch! Yes, I taught my children how to defang

those mechanical snakes, but most children won't have that knowledge. "Don't touch" is the safest, most logical thing for the public child education setting.

Leave the area! Bullets reach a long ways. If your kid isn't the only one there, he or she may not be able to overcome another child's impetuous desire to handle the "forbidden fruit" avatar of adult powers and responsibilities.

Tell an adult! Actually, this should probably read, "Tell a responsible adult," but that's probably too much conditional branching for a little kid.

There is a fascinating history behind this protocol, one that deserves to be better known. In the latter 1980s, Terry Mangan, then Chief of Police in Spokane, Washington, was a leader in public safety programs. He picked experts as advisors. One was Bob Smith, a firearms instructor in the civilian sector who was also a firefighter-paramedic. Looking at gun safety education, Bob flashed back to a program developed by the Jacksonville, Florida, Fire Department to combat incidents of kids being hurt playing with blasting caps found at construction sites. That protocol – Stop! Don't touch! Leave the area! Tell an adult! – had worked very well in that arena. It was soon adopted in Spokane for firearms accident prevention training. During the Spokane project, Smith had reached out to the National Rifle Association for input, and NRA in turn had asked to look at whatever the Spokane think tank came up with. Smith obligingly sent them "Stop! Don't touch! Leave the area! Tell an adult!"

I do not know at this writing, nor does Bob Smith, whether the Eddie Eagle mantra came from that, or whether it was separately discovered by such NRA stalwarts as Marion Hammer, who lived in Florida and would have had access to the Jacksonville information. Bob doesn't think it matters who came up with it, only that it works. I concur.

By the way, I've found an easy way to get adults to memorize it so they can pass it on to their kids: "Fellas, think of it as what your lady says to you when you look at another woman. 'Stop! Don't touch! Leave the area! Tell a responsible adult!'"

Hey, if something makes people smile or even laugh, they're likely to remember it, and remembering it is a key goal in any form of education.

CHAPTER FOUR

SAFETY AND GUN ACCIDENTS

What Went Wrong?

We cannot discuss gun safety without discussing how firearms accidents happen. The history of humanity is that we cannot defeat things we do not understand.

First, let's define our terms.

In recent years, those who would prohibit civilian owner-ship of firearms figured out that "gun control" wasn't selling as well as they had hoped. One approach they took to re-branding was to change the name of their product: now it was "gun violence" they wanted to control.

That did not turn out terribly well. New York City Mayor Michael Bloomberg, a vehement anti-gun activist, dipped into his billions and funded a bus full of anti-gun advocates to trav-el around the country preaching his sermon in assorted town squares. That fell on its face when, in reading off the victims of gun violence to a crowd in Concord, New Hampshire, the prohibitionists included in their toll would-be cop-killers who were shot by police in self-defense, *and the terrorist Tsarnev who had recently perpetrated the Boston Marathon bombing atrocity.* (To add spice to the Bloomberg-inspired cluelessness, his minions had apparently ignored that some said Tsarnev might have survived the wounds inflicted by police bullets, had his terrorist brother not run over him in the getaway car in his haste to escape.)

What to do? Why, the prohibitionists fell back to another strategy to re-brand their message: "We just want to promote gun safety."

Their idea of gun safety is: eliminate guns.

Well, let's see. We could certainly eliminate automobile fatalities by simply eliminating automobiles from society. But, wait: buses crash too, and so do trains, and of course, airplanes. Is it too late to go back to horses for transportation? But, wait again – don't horses have a long history of trampling people and kicking their owners to death? "After all, if it saves one life," is the mantra.

By that standard, we'd soon be back to caveman days, and walking everywhere…and people would still trip and fall and die. Forgive the *reduction ad absurdium,* but that really began with the childishly simplistic suggestion that banning guns was the painless, costless way to stop gun accidents.

The gun, like the automobile, is a power tool. The gun has been with us longer than the motor vehicle or the chain saw. It is a fact of life. Like any power tool, it is potentially dangerous. It is dealt with through responsible ownership and stewardship.

ACCIDENTAL OR NEGLIGENT?

When I came on the firearms scene, an unintended discharge of a firearm was known as an AD: an Accidental Discharge. I was already in the firearms industry when the paradigm changed. That new paradigm, today the mainstream in firearms training, is this: "If it was caused by a mechanical failure of the firearm, it was an Accidental Discharge, but if it was caused by anything else it was a Negligent Discharge (ND)!"

As best as I can determine, this meme was born in the firearms training academies sponsored by gun manufacturers. It was a time when the gun industry was under siege from often-unmeritorious lawsuits intended to put them out of business. I can understand why the manufacturers' lawyers would want to push an automatic assumption of negligence onto the end-user. They apparently succeeded: "If the gun didn't break, it was a negligent discharge" has gone mainstream in the firearms training world today.

I am sorry, but I cannot swim in that mainstream. I have been involved in the criminal justice system since 1972, and in the civil justice system since the 1980s. I have been arresting officer, police department prosecutor, and expert witness for the prosecution and on the civil side, for the plaintiff. I have been expert witness for police and civilian defendants in shooting cases and negligent discharge allegations. And these decades of experience have taught me this:

You don't automatically determine guilt or negligent culpability until you have investigated the damn case, seen all the evidence, and listened to both sides!

Certainly, there are cases where the discharge was negligent. When that is determined, we then backtrack and determine what led to the negligence. Intoxication? Ignorance? Arrogance? Bad training? Those factors do indeed come into play in the genuine negligent discharges.

But, often, the human failure that caused the discharge lay outside the person holding the gun. Let me ask you a question.

Have you ever been involved in an automobile accident? If so, was the accident caused by your vehicle's brakes failing, or a blown-out tire that jerked you out of your lane of travel? If so, by the standard stated above, it was indeed an accident.

Was your collision caused by something else, though? An animal or even a person ran in front of you, and you *had* to swerve or cause death? Perhaps another driver ran a red light and T-boned your car, or your vehicle skidded on snow or invisible "black ice"? If that's the case, I don't think you were negligent or at fault in any way. A jury that judges you, after being apprised of all the facts, probably won't think so either. And I bet YOU don't think so.

But, you have to realize, under the standard of "if the gun didn't mechanically malfunction, it's automatically considered a negligent discharge," then in any of the car crash scenarios I just described, *you are automatically deemed to be negligent, and at fault.*

Let's look at some ways in which something not your fault can be turned against you when someone is shot who didn't deserve to be shot.

EXTRANEOUS FAULT

I'll call it **Case One**. I was hired as an expert witness to address the grand jury in a shooting where the prosecution in Georgia was looking at a Felony Aggravated Assault charge against a police officer. He had chased an offender who was fleeing from police and had nearly run over an innocent victim. Like so many in the criminal subculture, he ran home to hide. He pulled into the driveway and ran to the front door of the home where he lived with his mom, and the cop pulled in right behind him and chased him on foot. It is law enforcement protocol that a drawn gun is allowed at the end of any pursuit of a person who won't stop for police, on the solidly logical theory that if he's willing to risk his own life and the lives of others in a high speed chase, he's very likely a bad guy with something to hide and willing to sacrifice a cop's life to escape. So, the officer had his service sidearm in his hand when he caught up to Sonny on the front porch outside the door.

Sonny wanted to fight. In a moment, Mommy burst out the door and grabbed at the officer's gun hand, digging her fingernails into his hand like claws. He tightened his grip in a startle response, and a shot was fired. It struck Sonny in the face, causing enough damage to make him look like the

Phantom of the Opera once the surgeons were done fixing him. Mommy told the police and the prosecutors that he had deliberately cocked the hammer of his handgun, pressed it hard into Sonny's face, and pulled the trigger out of pure malice.

The gunshot residue on Sonny's face showed that the muzzle had been a few inches away when the shot had been fired, and testing showed that had it been in muzzle contact, the violent blast of the .357 round would have caused much more damage than it did, and probably resulted in death. A smart cop on the scene that night took pictures of the officer's hand, and the claw marks from Mommy's deeply-digging fingernails were starkly present. It became clear to the grand jury that if Mommy hadn't grabbed the cop's hand and sunk in her fingernails, the shot probably would not have been fired. The grand jury returned "no true bill," in effect ruling that there was no reason to believe the officer had committed a crime.

Analysis: The officer had acted as he was trained. The grand jury's ruling was correct. Extraneous forces had caused the unintended discharge.

Case Two, Ohio. Multiple officers have pursued a stolen van, which finally pulls over. In an obviously rehearsed strategy, the four car thieves inside bail out and run in four different directions. The soon-to-be-defendant officer chases one of them, gun in hand as department policy suggests for such felony stops. Holding his 9mm out to the side away from the large male suspect, the cop grabs him by the back of the clothing with his free hand. Flailing wildly, the suspect's right hand strikes the pistol, and a shot is fired. The bullet strikes the suspect in the head, killing him instantly.

The dead car thief turns out to be in his early teens. While the officer is cleared by the criminal justice system, the family of the deceased files a lawsuit, alleging wrongful death.

My research and analysis showed that the officer had been taught to hold his service pistol with his thumb straight, pointed toward the muzzle. The flailing hand of the suspect came in from the right, striking the front of the slide and driving the front of the gun leftward. The officer's straight thumb was parallel to the trigger. The impact of the young suspect's hand hitting the gun did two things: it drove the gun the officer had been holding far to the right, far left…into direct alignment with the suspect's head. At the same time, it twisted the pistol inside the right hand to the left, bringing the trigger into violent contact with the officer's thumb and…BANG!

In a "perfect storm" of events the officer could not possibly have anticipated, the suspect's own actions had driven the striker-fired pistol's trigger against the thumb, causing the shot to be fired into his own head.

Shortly after I gave a sworn deposition to plaintiff's counsel, the plaintiffs decided to accept a settlement. The officer went back to his career. Nothing could bring back the young man who had died as a result of his own bad choices that began with participating in grand theft auto, and ended with an unintended gunshot that he could not have anticipated, either.

Case Three occurred in Canada. The officer had arrested a man who, as the constable drove into the police station, managed to jump out of the car and run. The officer drew his gun as he pursued on foot (he had reason to believe the suspect might become violent) and when the man suddenly spun toward him, he raised his weapon toward that suspect. A shot was fired and the suspect fell, mortally wounded. The officer stated that he didn't mean to fire, that the gun just "went off."

A charge of manslaughter ensued. Witnesses had stated that the gun appeared to be cocked, and that the officer had a shocked, surprised look on his face when the weapon discharged. I was hired as an expert witness by defense counsel.

As I dug into the case, I learned two things. One was that the police department in question bought cheap uniform gear on low bid, and had outfitted their officers with a crappy holster, the safety strap of which did not cover the hammer area of the hammer-fired service weapon. The police officers' association in that city offered evidence that they had complained about this, having noted that sometimes when seated in the patrol cars, the sleeves of their heavy winter coats would catch the hammer of the weapon and cock it in the holster. They had even seen the same thing happen when the officer's elbow went back against the hammer while they were wearing short-sleeved summer uniforms.

At that time, Canadian police training had lapsed far behind American police training in terms of firearms. I learned from the records that this officer had come on the department at a time when they were told to cock their hammers for range shooting at their Academy.

Had the officer become a victim of bad, obsolete training – what we call today a "training scar" – and reflexively cocked the hammer when he drew? Or had his weapon become cocked in the holster as had happened to other officers on his department?

My testimony in the Canadian court was that, within the totality of the evidence, one or the other of those scenarios was the most likely. In the end, the Canadian criminal justice system agreed, and the constable was ultimately exonerated.

The department involved went to all double action only

guns that *couldn't* be cocked to "hair trigger" status, intentionally *or* inadvertently, and finally bought good, modern holsters for its officers.

Had those preventative measures been in place beforehand, I honestly don't think this shooting would have occurred at all. The young felony suspect would have been alive with a chance to change his ways, and the policeman who never intended to launch the fatal shot would not have gone through a living hell, either.

Case Four, Michigan. A rookie cop is the youngest of three members of a university police department on patrol this night. He is riding with his field training officer. The third cop, a senior veteran of the job, is on patrol elsewhere on campus.

That third officer is making a routine arrest when the suspect turns on him violently, one handcuff clamped to his wrist and the other hanging free. He snatches the cop's handgun from his holster, and escapes. The stress is evident in the officer's voice when he broadcasts what happened and says desperately, "He's got my gun!"

The young rookie's heart is pounding as he and his FTO spot the suspect, pull him over, and take him at gunpoint. The FTO covered down on the suspect, and ordered the rookie to move forward and handcuff the suspect, who was now "proned out" as ordered and offering no further resistance.

When he emerged from the patrol car, the rookie had cocked the hammer of his issue service revolver, putting the trigger in the easily-released single action mode which many consider a hair trigger. At the Academy, he had been taught to cock the hammer whenever he might "have to make a critical shot." It apparently was never explained to him that the instructors probably meant a very long range shot or a very accurate one. However, the cop knew this terrifying person in front of him had just overpowered and nearly killed a much older and more seasoned "one of him." It sounded "critical" to him, and he said that was why he cocked the .38.

Reaching the suspect, the rookie kept the gun on him with one hand as he knelt on the man's shoulder to keep him down. He attempted to finish the handcuffing the first officer had started. But, when his left hand closed on the handcuff, the fingers of his right hand sympathetically tightened, too … and one of those fingers was on the trigger of a cocked service revolver.

The blast of the gunshot split the night. The bullet struck the surrendered suspect in the back and killed him almost instantly.

Outrage followed. "Helpless, unarmed, handcuffed man shot in back and murdered by police." The prosecutorial system didn't see the malice required for a murder charge, but felt they saw ample negligence, a key ingredient for a manslaughter case, and the young officer was so charged and indicted.

When he went to trial, defense attorney Bill Fette brought out the fact that the officer had, in his mind, done what he was trained to do. If there was negligence, the defense made clear, it was on the part of the employing agency and its training, not the individual officer who now stood accused.

It was the early 1990s. The state of tactical firearms training and firearms safety training was not yet what it is now. A leading law enforcement textbook on officer survival training included many photos of cops with guns drawn and fingers on triggers, even of fingers going to triggers during the draw. A recent hit movie had swept America, "The Silence of the

Lambs" with Jodie Foster playing a young special agent of the FBI. The FBI Academy scenes were filmed at the FBI Academy itself with the Bureau's obvious approval, and remember, the FBI Academy has long been to American law enforcement as Harvard Business School is to the nation's financial community. Presumably, those who made that film had access to FBI technical advisors. Yet, when she is facing a killer as Agent Starling in the movie, the supposedly well-coached Jodie Foster *cocks the hammer of her revolver* moments before shooting the serial murderer to death.

The standard of judgment in such cases has always been, "What would a reasonable, prudent person have done, in the same situation, knowing what the defendant knew?" The police version of that comes from the US Supreme Court's decision in *Graham v. Connor* and asks essentially, "What would a reasonable, prudent, trained and experienced police officer have done, in the same situation, knowing what that officer knew?"

This, apparently, is the standard the jury applied to the young Michigan officer. It was not unreasonable for him to have interpreted "cock the hammer for a critical shot" as he did. His training was not yet complete – indeed, he was undergoing field training at the time of the shooting – and by definition, he was not yet experienced.

Taking all that into consideration, the jury found him not guilty.

Whether the department was negligent to train him as he did was something else again. It was not the first accidental discharge due to interlimb response when a cop tried to do something forcible with one hand while holding a gun in the other. It would not be the last. While avoiding single action cocking and even mandating double action only weapons was already happening in many places, it was not yet the universal standard for the profession.

Thus, the department might have been able to argue that if their training was not cutting edge "best practices" in these respects, it was at least "within the mainstream of common custom and practice," and therefore did not fall to a substandard level. Today, of course, such training almost certainly WOULD be found to be substandard.

Another "cocked gun hair trigger accidental fatality" incident of note is **Case Five**, which occurred many years ago in a major Eastern city. A successful young businessman was driving about in his leased Ferrari with the son of a business associate. Suddenly, they were rammed in a hit-and-run by a couple of heroin junkies in a battered old Chevrolet. Furious, the businessman followed the car to get its license plate number. When both vehicles came to a stop, one of the junkies jumped out and approached the open-top sports car, waving a two-foot long police baton and uttering threats. The businessman was able to drive away.

He went around the block, thinking his antagonists would be gone by then. They weren't, and there was a second attempted assault by the club wielder. Again, the victim escaped by driving away, this time heading for his apartment. He had suffered a hit-and-run in the past, and knew that in this city, police would not be sent to investigate; he would have to get his paperwork, go to the local precinct house, and make a report. When he picked up the document, he also armed himself with the snub-nose .38 revolver he was licensed to carry; after all, he had just been repeatedly subjected to armed assault.

On the way to the police station, he spotted the offending vehicle parked on the street. Pulling over the Ferrari, he told his young companion to call the police while he kept an eye on the old Chevy.

Suddenly, the two junkies reappeared, across the street and on foot. One was still holding the 24-inch club, and making menacing gestures. His eyes locked on the businessman in recognition.

Seeing what was about to happen, the businessman drew his .38 and shouted for the bludgeon-wielder to stay back. At the single, simple firearms safety course he had ever attended, he had learned that he hit better single action than double action, and he cocked the hammer.

The doper screamed "I've been looking for you, fucker!" and, raising the club, began to charge across the street. Involuntarily, the businessman flinched back.

And his finger flinched on the trigger.

A 158 grain lead bullet sped across the street, striking the assailant in the forehead with fatal result. His accomplice froze in place. The businessman panicked, jumped into his Ferrari, and fled.

By the time he came to his senses and turned himself in, the media had already made the case a *cause celebre,* and the tabloid newspapers had dubbed the businessman "the Ferrari killer." He had fled the scene, in a world where flight has been seen as indicia of guilt since pre-Biblical times. The Bible says, in Proverbs 28:1, "The wicked flee where no man pursueth, but the righteous man stands his ground as bold as a lion." Much later, the US Supreme Court would phrase that a little differently. In the SCOTUS decision in *Illinois v. Wardlow* Chief Justice William Rehnquist wrote, "Headlong flight—wherever it occurs—is the consummate act of evasion: it is not necessarily indicative of wrongdoing, but it is certainly suggestive of such."

The short form is: "flight equals guilt."

The die was cast: this case would go to trial. The charge was murder.

The defense was that the discharge was accidental. I tried to convince the attorney to go to a straight self-defense plea, and was not the only one who urged that, but the attorney was the one calling the shots.

The defendant's case wasn't underway long before the judge ruled out any mention of self-defense. The defense was prepared to show that from the 32-foot distance which separated the two men at the time the shot was fired, the assailant could have closed that distance and crushed the defendant's skull with his deadly weapon in little more than two seconds. That was kept out, on the grounds that justifiability was a defense reserved for intentional acts, and incompatible with the "it was just an accident" theory of the defense. The deceased had previously committed multiple acts of violence – he had once so savagely beaten his crippled baby sister that his mother had kicked him out of the house – but none of that would come in either. Under Federal Rule of Evidence 404(b), prior bad acts of your opponent can not be used in defense of you for harming him, it they were not known to you at the time you took the action for which you are being judged.

Left with only the defense of "the gun went off by accident," the advocates for the defendant were handicapped. The jury returned a verdict of depraved murder. A later court of appeals reduced it to manslaughter, but the businessman served several years in prison and remains a convicted felon.

Virtually every professional who has analyzed the case believes that if he had not cocked the gun, had intentionally fired in self-defense, and stood his ground to explain himself afterward, he probably would never have been charged at all.

There are many takeaways from this case. One lesson, of course, is "Don't flee the scene." But the topic of this book is gun safety and preventing gun accidents, and in that regard, the big lessons are as follows.

First, *there is no such thing as a justifiable accident.* The best face that can ever be put on an accident is "excusable." What is the difference between "justifiable" and "excusable"? In a verdict of "justifiable" or "justified," the triers of the facts are essentially saying, "You did the right thing. You did the appropriate thing, and the outcome is acceptable." But in a verdict of "excusable," what's being said is, "This shouldn't have happened, but under the circumstances, any reasonable and prudent person would very likely have made the same mistake. Therefore, the mistake can be excused."

Second, this case is but a small part of a long history that cumulatively says, "Don't use a hair-trigger gun for any pursuit in which it is likely that you might be pointing a gun at a human being under stress."

There are shooting enthusiasts who love their light triggers, and argue that they'll be fine since they "keep their booger hooker off the bang switch." Unfortunately, this presumes that they are perfect people incapable of making a mistake. In one European study of highly trained SWAT-type personnel, they were issued pistols equipped with sensor switches hooked up to computers, and sent through a high-stress simulation exercise. When it was over, they were asked how many times they had touched their triggers. Most who said they never touched their triggers were shocked to find out how many times they had in fact done so. Their brain wasn't picking up on the touch, but the computer and the sensors were.

Certainly, it is important to go back to the rule we discussed earlier: THE FINGER WILL ONLY BE ON THE TRIGGER WHEN WE ARE IN THE VERY ACT OF INTENTIONALLY FIRING THE GUN. However, any kind of safety engineering must have safety nets. Firearms safety is no exception.

There is nothing in the "black letter law," the statutes and the codes, which specifies what is or is not a "hair trigger." The closest we have to it in caselaw was the holding of the Federal court of appeals in Case Five, that "the cocked hammer set to release at the slightest pressure" not a responsible thing to have in a gun pointed at a human being.

In that case, the trigger pull with the gun cocked was 4.5 pounds. Ironically, that would be "in spec" for the same manufacturer's single action service pistols, which are also provided with manual "safety catch" and grip safety. What makes a trigger pull of a certain weight "within spec" on one firearm, but "dangerously light" on the other?

It boils down to an issue of whether or not the given piece of equipment was properly adjusted in terms of safety. That in turn will come down to one or both of two elements. One is the manufacturer's own specification. The other would be the "common custom and practice" of adjusting such machines.

That would be the crux of the matter if the case involved a car whose brakes failed with the death of an innocent pedestrian or motorist resulting. Were the brakes properly adjusted as per the manufacturer's standards? Were they in the same good order that a competent professional auto mechanic would adjust them to? The same would be true for a machine involved in an industrial accident in a factory…and the same is true of a firearm.

What is "common custom and practice"? That takes a while to evolve. Let's consider the 1911 genre of pistol, now in production and widespread use for well over a century. When adopted by the US military in March of 1911, the spec for the trigger pull weight was five to seven pounds. The single company that has manufactured them longest considers four pounds the absolute minimum for one that will be used as a "service pistol," i.e., a defense gun. The National Rifle Association sets a four-pound trigger pull limit on any 1911 used in their Distinguished Match. Clearly, a pattern emerges here: four pounds is probably the red-line bottom poundage on a defensive 1911.

There is also manufacturer specification. The Glock pistol is probably the most popular in America today, having been introduced to this country in the early-mid 1980s. It was introduced with a 5.5-pound trigger pull. In the late 1980s, Glock introduced a target pistol version with a lighter pull, advertised at 3.5 pounds. It would later be re-designated 4.5 pounds, but remained the exact same part. From the beginning, Glock sold this trigger ONLY on its dedicated target models. The company adamantly told its armorers (factory-trained repair people around the country) to NEVER install the 3.5/4.5-pound connector in a service pistol. (They later modified their policy to allow that part only if it was in company with the New York trigger spring. The NY-1 trigger, developed at the insistence of the New York State Police, gave a firmer resistance to the finger from the beginning of the trigger pull. In conjunction with the 3.5/4.5-pound connector, the result was a pull weight in the range of six pounds, which Glock found acceptable for safety. The NY-2 module, created for the New York City Police Department, makes the trigger pull heavier still.)

Some have been confused because Glock produces a series of pistols called the Tactical/Practical, which come with the 4.5-pound trigger. However, despite their name, they were designed originally for tactically- and practically-based action pistol shooting matches. Police departments which order them receive them shipped from the factory with the standard 5.5-pound trigger pulls. The Tactical/Practical models are not listed on the manufacturer's website or in their catalog under military or police service pistols or defense pistols, but as sport firearms.

Thus, we have a different pistol with a different design from a different manufacturer; ergo, the recommended pull weight is different. The person who ignores company policy, lightens the trigger pull, and is subsequently accused of a reckless, negligent accidental shooting, will now find himself in the impossible position of convincing a jury of people who aren't gun enthusiasts that he knew more about the pistol than the man who designed it and the company that has produced seven figures worth of them. Will that attitude defeat the other side's argument of arrogant recklessness, or assist it? Probably the latter.

Another thing that has to be remembered is that it is not unknown for an accidental shooting case to be falsely alleged.

FALSE ALLEGATIONS OF NEGLIGENCE

"It went off by accident" sounds to most people like a guilty man trying to mitigate his guilt, and bring his conviction down from murder to the lesser charge of manslaughter. While that has been known to happen, the strategy has also been used against people who legitimately and deliberately fired in self-defense.

How would that come about? Remember what we established earlier: "There is no such thing as a justifiable accident." But the prosecution knows that the affirmative defense of self-defense, if the jury is convinced, is a "perfect defense."

It is less important to the prosecutor to win a conviction for first degree murder instead of second degree, or any kind of murder instead of manslaughter, than it is to simply *win a conviction!* Any conviction is seen as a "win" for the prosecutor's office. But an acquittal is a public, professional humiliation, not to mention a tacit implication that the prosecutor in office may be wrongfully persecuting innocent people, which can be fatal to the job of the head of that office in the next election.

To win a prosecution for murder against the typical armed citizen who kills a criminal in self-defense is pretty tough. The jury will quickly see that the defendant is someone like them, a productive member of society with a clean record, kind of like the nice person who lives next door. It's hard to convince them that someone just like them can turn into a cold-blooded murdering monster.

But to win a conviction for manslaughter? That's a much easier sell. The key ingredient there is recklessness and negligence. It a world where any firearms instructor will have to testify that it's very easy for a light trigger pull gun to discharge, where soldiers don't consider "hair triggers" safe for soldiering and cops don't consider them safe for policing and most hunters don't consider them safe for hunting, will the use of such a trigger to take someone at gunpoint be seen as negligence?

Now all the prosecution has to do is argue a theory that you were negligent in pointing that hair trigger gun at the intruder who drunkenly stumbled into your house by accident. They'll say your gun went off through negligence, causing the terrible injury in question.

Sure, you'll say "I shot him intentionally, to keep him from killing me and my family!" But the other side will say, "Isn't it true you're so macho and full of yourself that you're just saying that because you can't admit you made a mistake?"

In a world where EVERYBODY makes mistakes, a theory that you did so becomes an easy sell…and your light trigger firearm plays right into the other side's hands.

On the civil lawsuit side, the motivation is different. The goal is generally to get money, which means that the plaintiff's lawyers suing you are looking for deep pockets. Most people don't have a million dollars laying around in a slush fund to satisfy a judgment against them for that amount. Lawyers don't try to get blood out of stones. But almost every homeowner has a million dollars worth of homeowner liability insurance, and any responsible driver has a million dollars worth of automobile liability insurance. *And the insurance company DOES have the money!*

Thus, for the plaintiff too, it becomes attractive to fabricate a theory of the case in which you recklessly, negligently pointed a hair-trigger gun at someone while in a state of high excitement…and discharged it by indefensible, negligent "accident." Now they're into the deep pockets of your homeowner's insurance carrier if you shot a home invader. Now they're into the deep pockets of the automobile liability carrier if you had to shoot a carjacker, or a man violently attacking you out of "road rage."

Set down this book now and go look up your own insurance

policies. Read the fine print. You'll see that the insurance companies are expressly exempt from having to pay off on what is called a willful tort, your deliberate act which harms another. That's why they won't say you did it deliberately. It gives them a hook on which to hang their case, and an open avenue to the insurance company's rich coffers.

Is their allegation BS? Yes, it is. But you have to understand that what you and I would consider BS becomes, when uttered by an attorney, "the opposing party's theory of the case." It has to be treated in court as if it is every bit as valid as the truth you are trying to get across to the jury.

BOGUS ALLEGATIONS

I've been involved in fighting bogus allegations of negligence for thirty years as I write this. That first case thirty years ago came about in a video arcade in a large city in the Southeast, where two police officers were arresting a 20-year old man for illegal possession of a firearm. It was once again a field training officer and a rookie.

The FTO proactively drew his gun with his right hand and held it up where the suspect could see it. He placed his left hand on the man's shoulder to hold him in position, and told the rookie to get the gun. As he made eye contact with the rookie, the suspect apparently saw that the senior officer's eyes were off him for the moment, and that's when he made his move.

He spun toward the officer, reaching under his sweater for his gun.

The cop shot him in the head and killed him before he could pull it out. It turned out to be a stolen .22 caliber revolver loaded with hyper-velocity hollow point ammunition.

It was a cross-racial shooting in a city already riven with racial tension. What was now **Case Six** triggered an epic race riot, the second largest in that beleaguered city's history. The city needed a scapegoat.

The officer was charged with manslaughter.

The state's theory of the case was that the officer had cocked the hammer of his service revolver, to show off as if he was emulating a Dirty Harry movie, and that he was startled and accidentally shot the young man in the head. Inspection of the gun showed that two coils had been removed from the trigger return spring at some time. The officer adamantly testified that he had fired the one shot intentionally, double action, because he knew the suspect had a gun, and was going for it with the obvious intent of killing him and his rookie partner.

The prosecution couldn't find a police instructor who would testify to what they wanted, so they brought in an expert witness who testified that the slightly altered trigger return spring had made the gun "more lethal, with greater firepower." They also brought in a thirteen year old boy who, as an eyewitness, testified that the gun was cocked.

When my turn came as an expert witness for the defense, I explained that removing two coils from the trigger return spring was an approved modification for service weapons at that manufacturer's armorer's school, and that the weaker spring slowed down trigger return. This *reduced* the firepower by reducing the speed at which the trigger could re-set for the next shot. Firepower in terms of ammunition capacity was not affected, of course, because it was a six-shot revolver. Nor did it matter to lethality: that was a function of the ammunition, and the officer was using regulation, department issue hollow points. I explained that, for many reasons, it was my opinion that he had not cocked the revolver, and had intentionally fired it double action.

During cross examination, the prosecutor asked if I was familiar with the testimony of the boy. I replied that I was. He said, "So, you don't believe in eyewitness testimony?" I replied, "Sir, under the circumstances, I cannot accept the testimony of A------ B---." He then asked the question some professor in law school must have taught him not to ask: "Why?"

I replied, "Sir, A----- B--- is thirteen years of age. He has less than the common knowledge of firearms. He has testified that he had never even seen a real gun except on TV or in a passing policeman's holster, until this night – in the dark – a measured thirty-three feet away – through the tinted glass of the video arcade window. It is clear from his deposition that he didn't know what it WAS to 'cock a revolver' until you, sir, showed him in your office. It is also clear from his deposition that he was led to believe that the revolver HAD to be cocked to fire. He has seen the flash, he has heard the shot, he has seen (the deceased) stiffen and fall, and someone had led him to believe that the gun had to be cocked for that to happen. For all those reasons, sir, I cannot accept the testimony of A------ B---."

That pretty much ended that avenue of cross examination, and to make a long story short, the officer was found not guilty by a jury that deliberated for only about two hours after eight months of testimony and argument, then the longest criminal trial in that state's history. When the verdict was announced, the city had its third largest race riot, but that may be the price a city pays for electing spineless politicians to positions of power, from which they can throw innocent people to the wolves.

Between the shooting and the trial, that city recalled every issue service revolver and had its armorers convert them to double action only so they couldn't be cocked at all.

I submit that if the city had done that before the shooting ever happened, the prosecutors would not have had that fragile peg on which to hang their bogus case at all.

MECHANICAL FAILURES

The so-called "true accidental discharge" occurs when some mechanical malfunction of the weapon causes a shot to be fired, or when the gun blows up. These incidents are rare, but they do happen.

That mechanical problem may be induced by human error on the part of the user. For what I'll call **Case Seven**, let's go back in time to the Western Frontier in the late Nineteenth Century, in the Oklahoma Territory. One of the most famous lawmen of that place and time was Bass Reeves. Some said he was the first black Federal Marshal, and he was certainly the first African-American appointed by the famous "hanging judge," Isaac Parker. Famous for his skill with handgun and rifle alike, Marshal Reeves had occasion to kill fourteen men in gunfights. A deeply religious man himself, he was able to cope with that. What haunted him to the end of his days was the fifteenth man he killed, because it happened by accident. Here's what I had to say about it when I wrote his story in the Ayoob Files, a continuing feature in *American Handgunner* magazine.

"It has been noted that for much of his career, Reeves preferred to carry revolvers and rifles of the same caliber. It wasn't just about ammo logistics for him, it was also about hard experience. In 1884 beside a campfire, he discovered he had mistakenly loaded a .45 Colt revolver cartridge into his .44-40 Winchester. Trying to pry the jammed round out of the magazine with his pocket knife, he accidentally discharged the rifle. The bullet struck his cook in the neck, mortally wounding him. Reeves was subsequently tried for murder. Though acquitted at trial, his substantial legal expenses depleted his life savings and left him financially hurting for the rest of his life. (Some things don't change over the centuries…)"

It is likely that this was human error-based, but a mechanical malfunction was involved. That malfunction was in turn, however, induced by the human error of putting the wrong caliber cartridge in the firearm. Working in the flickering light of the fire with only a pocketknife, Reeves was very likely so focused on the close-up detail work of what he was doing that the gun's muzzle was allowed to stray in an unsafe direction. A round must have been in the firing chamber, and something very likely hit the trigger. With all the participants long dead and written documentation scant, it's not possible to do the sort of full investigation that we would do with a fresh incident today.

It is a fact, however, that things other than pulling the trigger can cause a loaded firearm to discharge. Earlier in this book, we've had the discussion about inertia-firing with dropped guns or guns that are struck hard on either end. Let's go to **Case Eight**, which occurred a century after Bass Reeves' tragic fatal incident, with a similar rifle.

The gun was an extremely popular .30-30 lever action rifle, which had been in production since the late Nineteenth Century. Millions of them had been produced. It became "America's rifle" before the AR15 did. A young man was out hunting with one when he slipped and fell, hard. So, of course, did the rifle. It discharged, wounding multiple hunters in his party. A lawsuit was filed against the manufacturer.

I was approached by plaintiffs' counsel to be an expert

witness. I told him what I tell all lawyers who make that approach: I won't take a case unless I've reviewed all the discovery, and am convinced that the retaining party is in the right. I further told him that I was extremely skeptical about his case, since I had hunted deer with a rifle like that off and on since I was a little boy.

I became convinced. Through the course of discovery, we learned that with a round in the chamber and the hammer on half-cock, a sharp blow to the lever could indeed cause the heavy firing pin to go forward with enough impact to discharge the weapon. I was stunned. Documents the court ordered the manufacturer to give the plaintiffs showed that this had been known to happen as far back as the early Twentieth Century, and the manufacturer was well aware of it! Internal memos indicated that changing production would be more expensive than paying a settlement on the occasional lawsuit, so the matter was buried and nothing was done about it.

The manufacturer lost big time in court. The rifle's design was changed, incorporating a lighter firing pin, a heavier firing pin spring, and a manual safety to boot. Having used the original version of that gun since I was a little kid – it was the first high-powered rifle I ever fired – I frankly felt betrayed.

BLOW-UPS

Yes, guns can explode. It is very rare, but it does happen. Usually, there was some human error that went into it. An example is the .308 Winchester cartridge mistakenly bolted into a .270 Winchester chamber, described in an earlier chapter, which blew up a fine sporting rifle and caused some permanent injury to the careless shooter who was involved.

Just as hospitals now refer to dead patients as "bad outcomes" or "negative outcomes," blown-up guns are euphemistically referred to in the firearms industry as "catastrophic events." Colloquially, they're sometimes called a "kB," short for "ka-BOOM." I believe that term was coined by my old friend Dean Speir, an iconoclastic and consumer-oriented gun writer.

The majority of these that I've personally encountered were due to human error: bad handloads. The person recycling their spent brass to produce their own re-made cartridges sometimes used the wrong gunpowder. More often, they simply put in too much of the right gunpowder. This is why smart handloaders try to select a loading "recipe" that uses a powder sufficiently bulky that if the machine (or the brain) should malfunction and a double dose is dumped in, it will spill over and prevent a bullet from being seated over it.

Bad factory rounds do occur, but they're extraordinarily rare. I know two men who lost strong guns to one bad lot of .45 caliber +P ammunition, a Colt Government Model and a Glock 21. The red-faced boutique manufacturer of the ammo quickly replaced both firearms that were ruined in these

Cases Nine and Ten.

In 1990, the .40 Smith & Wesson cartridge was introduced by S&W and Winchester, and quickly became The Next Big Thing. Today, there are more police departments issuing pistols in this caliber than in any other. The .40 S&W is a high pressure cartridge, designed to work in pistols designed for the less powerful 9mm Luger round.

Before long, there were cases of "kB" happening, often with one particular brand of gun which had a barrel that did not fully support the chamber at the bottom rear. This meant that in that small area of the cartridge, when the gunpowder ignited there was only the brass of the cartridge case to contain it. This resulted in the occasional "case head separation" blow-up, which generally blasted the magazine out of the gun, often blew out the extractor, and occasionally destroyed barrel, slide, and frame. These occurred mostly with hot handloads. There were, however, a few with factory rounds. In **Case Eleven**, a major American manufacturer admitted fault and recalled a large amount of ammunition after this happened a few times with those cartridges. In **Case Twelve**, it happened in front of me on a police academy range while I was teaching a Lethal Threat Management for Police course. The officer wasn't seriously injured, but it stung his hand so badly by surprise that he dropped the now-ruined gun. The load in question was from a foreign factory, a 170 grain "IPSC Load" as the company called it. The ammo manufacturer apologized and paid for the gun. Soon that brand of pistol was being manufactured with more reinforcement in the case-head area of the barrel, and it has been a long time since I've heard of that happening with one of their guns and factory ammunition.

"Outsourcing" is increasingly popular in American manufacturing, and the firearms industry is no exception. It occasionally leads to problems. In 2005, one of the great old-line American gun companies introduced a new revolver caliber for hunting, designed to take *extremely* powerful ammunition. This stuff was running at a pressure range normally associated with high powered rifles. As a result, the new load had a very flat trajectory, and it also turned out to be stunningly accurate. I was one of the gun writers at the introduction, which included a hog hunt on the Brahma Island game preserve in Florida. These guns were so powerful that we often couldn't print pictures of the animals that were shot, in the gun magazines we wrote for. With a head shot, the result was so explosive there were evacuated skulls and enucleated eyeballs lying next to the instantly-killed animals.

Demand for these guns among hunters, once the word got out, was huge. Customers wanted various new models. When demand was seen for a short barrel version, the company was so back-ordered on their own production lines already that they contracted with a trusted European manufacturer to make the barrels.

They weren't out long before the first blow-up, **Case Thirteen**. The owner of the gun photographed a friend shooting it, and his motor-drive Nikon caught the barrel separating from the gun. Fortunately, no one was hurt. The manufacturer was extremely responsible about it: they issued an immediate recall on that run of guns, and both the shooter and the owner of the destroyed revolver got their pick of the company's finest and most expensive handguns as compensation.

These things can occur with smaller caliber firearms, too. I was the "victim" in **Case Fourteen** in the 1990s. A manufacturer was trying to produce a small pocket-size semiautomatic pistol in .22 Long Rifle that would be accurate, reliable, and hold more cartridges than competing manufacturers' guns of that type. They sent me a prototype to test.

It was indeed accurate, surprisingly so. (If you're going to use little, weak bullets for self-defense, you have to place them with surgical accuracy, so precision shooting capability was a key parameter of that design.) I tried it with standard velocity .22 Long Rifle ammo. It was utterly reliable and impressively accurate. "Cool," I thought. Then I tried some high velocity .22 Long Rifle loads. Same high orders of reliability and accuracy. "*Way* cool," I thought to myself.

Then I loaded a magazine of hyper-velocity ammunition,

chambered a round, indexed on the target, and started the trigger-pulling.

Wham! I was hit in the face by a hot, stinging blast, and a cloud of white smoke enveloped the gun and my hands. I removed my finger from the trigger guard, and lowered the little pistol, which was now in ruined condition. The open-top slide, made of solid ordnance steel, had bowed outward. The magazine had been blasted out of the bottom of the pistol.

Things looked kind of gray and fuzzy. That concerned me. I set down the pistol and took my glasses off. The polycarbonate lenses looked as if they had been sandblasted.

For the third time in my life, good glasses had saved my eyesight from a firearms mishap. The pistol had experienced a "kB" in the form of a case head separation. The gunmaker's objective had been to get reliable feeding with more cartridges in the magazine than the competition could fit into the same-size gun. The .22 Long Rifle cartridge has always been a nightmare for firearms designers, because it is relatively long and thin, and has a big rim at its rear. This alters the angle of the respective cartridges as they come up through the feed stack inside the magazine. When it comes each of those cartridges' turn to go into the chamber, they may be approaching at a slightly different angle.

Accordingly, in its quest to get more cartridges feeding 100% of the time, the engineers had given a very steeply-dished angle to the cartridge feed ramp. For this to work, some case head support had to be sacrificed. When the relatively very high pressure of the hyper-velocity cartridge went into effect, there was nothing but brass to contain it. The result was that "catastrophic event."

The gunmaker apologized profusely, paid for new glasses to

replace the ruined ones, and decided to be more conservative in their approach to firepower. By going one round less in capacity, they didn't have to make the feed ramp so steep, and now the case-head was better supported during the firing cycle. The pistol went on the market, remains there today, and to my knowledge has never been involved in another "catastrophic event."

BLOW-UPS IN PERSPECTIVE

All this discussion of guns blowing up could lead an unwary reader to believe that it was an everyday occurrence. *Au contraire.* These are extremely rare "black swan events." How rare are they? Literally *billions* of cartridges are fired on shooting ranges around the country and the world. Blown-up guns are so rare that they are practically headline news on the Internet when they occur.

THE ENEMY WITHIN

Gun safety failures include situations in which a dangerous person has somehow gained access to the firearms lawfully purchased and responsibly owned by some good citizen. This is an issue that cannot be ignored in a book on gun safety.

What I call "the enemy within" is someone in the inner circle of the responsible people who is, himself, irresponsible.

Case Fifteen: On December 14, 2012, twenty-year-old Adam Lanza perpetrated one of the most horrendous crimes in American history. He gained access to a .22 caliber rifle his mother had lawfully purchased. He shot her with it four times, killing her. He was then able to access her gun safe. He showed up at the Sandy Hook Elementary School in Newtown, Connecticut. By then he had armed himself with an AR15 rifle and several magazines, a 10mm pistol and a 9mm pistol, and a semiautomatic shotgun which he left in the car. He shot his way into the school and murdered twenty helpless little children and six helpless adult victims, before police arrived and he shot himself to death with the 10mm.

His mother, the first victim, had known that her son had long had severe psychological problems. Those problems were escalating, and she was finally considering sending him away to where he could get help. It is believed by some close to the case that he got wind of those maternal intentions, and that this is what triggered his murder spree.

We treat our loved ones differently from others, if only because we feel responsible for them. We want to see the best in the people we love, and that leads us to blank out the worst.

We need to not do that. When there are signs that those loved ones are a danger to themselves and others, we need to do what psychologists and psychiatrists are bound to do with patients who manifest the same tendencies: we must report them and get professional help for them, and before we do anything else, render them harmless to others.

Anthony Lanza's mother did not do that, and she was the first to pay the terrible price for that refusal to see, to accept, what was coming.

If nothing else, it needs to be done for the troubled one himself. While the first victim of the Lanza atrocity was the killer's mother, it's easy to forget that the last to die by his hand was Adam Lanza himself.

Let's look to **Case Sixteen.** An elderly man suffered a stroke at age 79 which blew out the "inhibition centers" in his brain. It left him, essentially, as the equivalent of a man with advanced Alzheimer's disease. When he got out of the hospital, unable to care for himself, his adult son took him in to his home with his wife and young daughter.

It became apparent that the old man was now Someone Else, a person ruled by impulse, who had suddenly become prone to rage and violence. The son who had taken him in was a police officer with a substantial gun collection, who had to always have a handgun accessible because he was constantly on call by his police department, and couldn't simply leave the guns in a department locker. He removed all his firearms from his home, and stored them with relatives, except for his service sidearm and backup handgun. His dad's lack of inhibition made him quickly realize that the normal boundaries were gone. He learned to keep his service weapon on his person at all times at home, in a concealment holster, and the backup gun strapped to his own leg in an ankle holster.

The situation degenerated. Knives had to be removed from the kitchen. The son and his wife sent their daughter to live with her maternal grandparents until they could get things sorted out. But, they didn't sort well. When the brain-damaged father attacked the son's wife physically, the time came to institutionalize his father. The decision had a profound emotional and economical impact, but it proved to be the right thing to do. In the end, no one was hurt.

Contrast that with **Case Seventeen.** A young husband helplessly watched his wife descend into self-destructive madness. The day came when she attempted suicide with one of his guns, but she was interdicted and institutionalized. The young husband removed all the guns from his house.

The time came, several months later, when it seemed that she had "normalized." After a while, because there had been rising crime in the neighborhood, she told him she'd feel safer if he brought the guns back into the house. He had missed his beloved hobby…she seemed "all right now" … and he brought the guns back in. Back when she had been "normal," she had been recoil sensitive, so he had handloaded some very mild .38 Special cartridges to load in the .357 Magnum revolver that once again went into the bedroom for home security purposes.

The night came when she began acting strangely, and left him alone in the living room. He went to see where she was, and found her standing in front of the bedroom mirror holding that revolver to her head. He tried to grab it out of her hand… she jerked violently away…and a shot was fired. The bullet went into her brain and killed her.

He called the police, of course. The investigation showed no gunshot residue (GSR) on her head. The fired spent casing was that of a +P .38 Special, which lab testing showed should have left GSR. He tried to explain that, no, it was a light handload; later testing by his defense team showed that at the distance involved, that round very likely would not have left GSR. But, because rules of evidence demand independent confirmation of what was in the gun in such circumstances, and this was now a case of "the defendant manufactured the evidence," those facts did not go in front of the jury. The authorities believed she must have been shot from a greater distance by the only person who could have done so, the husband. After a long three-trial ordeal, he was convicted for manslaughter and served a term in prison.

A young woman dead, and a young man bankrupted and destroyed. While this case is best known among gun enthusiasts as an argument as to whether or not handloaded ammunition should be used in defensive firearms, it is also very much an example of why, when there is an enemy within – an evil member of the family who might commit atrocious mass murder, or a broken member of the family who might attempt suicide – the balance of competing harms and needs tells us to make firearms totally inaccessible to those loved ones.

My first reaction when the defense lawyers called me about Case Seventeen was that if someone was stupid enough to leave a loaded gun where a known suicidal person could reach it, they probably WERE guilty of manslaughter…but then I had to look at the fact that the loved ones of substance abuse sufferers and the mentally ill are so grateful when there is the "calm in the storm" that makes their loved one seem normal again, they desperately want to believe that.

It turns out to be a siren song. As much as we want to believe that they're no longer a danger to themselves and others, we simply can't – for their sake, and for our own sake, and for the sake of others.

THE IMPORTANCE OF SELF-ANALYSIS

We have to remember that we are all the imperfect children of imperfect parents in an imperfect world, and that none of us is ever immune to making a mistake. I would be remiss if I did not close this book with the one negligent discharge I've been personally responsible for. Consider it **Case Eighteen.**

It was the late 1970s, and I was preparing for a national championship in Colorado. Our pistol team decided that we would replicate some of the expected courses of fire on our own turf, and held a match for that purpose. One stage was called "Guatemalan Steakhouse," and it presumed that we were in a restaurant eating dinner when terrorists came in, opened fire, and wounded us in the gun arm. Strangely, we were allowed to "stage" the gun under a linen dinner napkin, so our non-dominant hand could reach it, as if we knew we were going to get shot in the gun arm. But, anyway…

I was one of those running the match, and since the shoemaker's children go barefoot, I didn't have a chance to practice it myself. When my turn came, since I didn't have an ambidextrous safety on my Colt .45 auto, I made the spur of the moment decision to lower the hammer on a live round and cock the gun when I brought it up. The start signal came, and watching the target instead of my hand, I grabbed the gun and went to cock it and – BANG!

There was actually time to think, "Who fired that shot? I'm the only one on the shooting bay!" And then, in slow motion, I saw my trusted, familiar pistol in midair, arcing its muzzle across the length of my body until it landed between my feet. I reflexively stepped on it as if it was a poisonous snake. Someone said "Oh… my…God!" And someone else (kindly, I realize now in retrospect) blurted "Of all people…"

Reconstruction showed what had happened. Someone said the linen (actually, a diaper; our shooting team didn't have any linen dinner napkins) had caught between my finger and the trigger. Whether that was true or not, I was the one who had somehow applied pressure to the trigger. That particular pistol had a BoMar rear sight that extended back past the slide, leaving a tenuous grasp of the thumb on the hammer spur. The hammer had slipped out from under the thumb; the trigger was undoubtedly back, and – a mistake I never made again – I had deactivated the grip safety because a gun guru had told me it was the right thing to do.

Analysis: Negligent discharge. The human error of arrogant overconfidence. Even though I always carried that gun cocked and locked and had no experience thumbing the hammer back on a live round, especially with my non-dominant hand, I had been shooting that kind of gun since age 12 and considered it an extension of my hand. I was watching the target to get a faster sight picture, instead of looking at my hand and watching what I was doing.

The bullet went through the bridge table and into the ground a few inches ahead of my boot. I dug it out of the ground that day, and had it cast in Lucite to put on my trophy rack, so I'd be reminded of the price of *hubris*. The now-grungy bridge table, almost 40 years old, sits against the wall in my carport today with its ineradicable .45 caliber bullet hole, to remind me all these decades later that whenever I leave or come home, that responsibility for gun safety rides along with that pistol on my hip.

GUN SAFETY ITSELF IN PERSPECTIVE

Americans tend to be careful with their firearms. There will always be idiots who do stupid things. There will always be people who abuse the power they hold. It is true in the microcosm of the aberrant individual. And, when you look at some of the gun prohibitionist propaganda, it becomes apparent that it is also true among certain politicians, in macrocosm.

Those of us who abide by the law and own or even carry guns, whether by choice or by need, must always remember that power and responsibility are commensurate. Each must always be in equal balance. Never forget that equation: power without responsibility becomes tyranny, but responsibility without power is the very definition of futility.

Stay safe.

IN SUMMARY

We are all surrounded by things that make our lives better, but also carry danger with them. Take it from a decades-long frequent flier who survived an aircraft crash seven months prior to writing this. It comes with this dangerous thing we call Life.

The gun is merely a microcosm of this. Mankind has known through most of its epoch that fire is a wonderful servant and a fearful master. "Fire" is the first syllable of "firearm." Same, same.

At my schools, Lethal Force Institute from 1981 to 2009 and Massad Ayoob Group since, the word "safe" has been defined as an acronym. It stands for Secure, Asshole-Free Environment. People who do stupid things violate that definition of "safe," and that's why we kick the careless ones out. They simply don't belong in the company of the responsibly armed.

As we end this time together, I ask you to remember that while accidents can occur at any point on the bell curve of experience, I've found that with firearms they tend to cluster on both ends of that curve. On the one end, the newbies too irresponsible to learn before doing, and on the other, people so familiar with their potentially dangerous equipment that "familiarity bred contempt," and they fell into carelessness.

I've had the privilege of being mentored by many of the great gun people of my time. One of them advised me to treat my gun like a pet rattlesnake. I would be proud of my ownership of it and my ability to command it, he warned, but I must never forget that it was built to bite, and if I was the least bit careless with it, I would be the one person most often within its venomous range.

I took that advice to heart. So should you. We have these weapons to protect ourselves and the people we most love. We must never forget that they are the ones most likely to be near us – literally, sometimes, in the line of fire – when we handle those guns. When we load them, unload them, check them and clean them, put them on and put them away. We must never drop our guard with them. We need to treat them as if we were engineers, with safety net after safety net in place, and always a conscious focus on what we're doing with them, so they can be there and ready to perform their tasks, up to and including protecting our loved ones from the worst imaginable evil.

Massad Ayoob

ABOUT THE AUTHOR

Massad Ayoob has published thousands of articles in gun magazines, martial arts publications, and law enforcement journals, and authored more than a dozen books on firearms, self-defense, and related topics.

During his distinguished career, Ayoob has won several state and regional handgun shooting championships. He was voted by his peers Outstanding American Handgunner of the Year in 1998, won the Roy Rogers Award for promoting firearms safety and the James Madison Award for promoting Second Amendment rights, appeared as an expert witness for courts in weapons and shooting cases, and currently appears in numerous television shows.

He founded the Lethal Force Institute in 1981 and served as its director until 2009, and now trains through Massad Ayoob Group (http://massadayoobgroup.com).

GunDigest
SHOOTER'S GUIDE to
HANDGUNS

GRANT
CUNNINGHAM

SAFE TRANSPORT

When transporting firearms, it is important to know the laws that apply where you're traveling. In most cases, and in the absence of a concealed carry license, the law requires that handguns be transported unloaded in a locked container. That's a good start, but what about actually protecting those guns from theft?

Leaving a loaded, unsecured gun in a vehicle, even if it's out of sight, is irresponsible. Car prowls are one of the most common forms of crime in the country, and a handgun is a great prize for any thief. A handgun should never be kept, even for a very short period of time, in a glove compartment, center console, or under the seat.

The safest place for a gun is either a) on your person, or b) in a locked, secure container. There are a number of small safes that are designed expressly for mounting in a vehicle and feature brackets or mounting flanges to allow that. They usually mount to the floor and some can even be located under a seat. This allows you (or any of your passengers) to remove your gun and store it when necessary. They're especially handy for trips

A box of copier paper, restacked so that the reams face the target side, makes a safe dryfire backstop.

It's not responsible, or safe, to leave a gun in a glovebox or car console!

which include entry into areas where guns are off limits.

Be aware that having a lockbox mounted within reach of the driver may violate laws that require the gun and its container to be out of reach. Research the laws in your area carefully, and if in doubt contact your state or local gun rights organization.

If you're simply transporting guns to and from the range, most state's laws allow for them to be placed in hard-sided, locked containers and stored out of the immediate reach of the driver. Always unload all guns before putting them in any sort of storage boxes! There are incidents every year in which people are shot by loaded guns in storage containers, largely because their soft interiors - so prized for preventing damage and scratches - touch the trigger when they're closed. If the trigger is in contact with something, it doesn't take much to move it enough to fire. Unload the gun, make doubly sure that it's unloaded, and only then put it into the case or box.

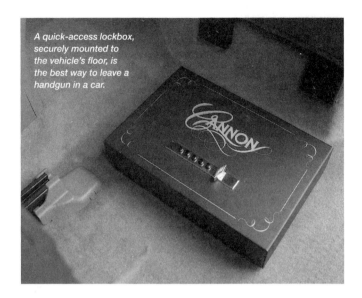

A quick-access lockbox, securely mounted to the vehicle's floor, is the best way to leave a handgun in a car.

DRYFIRING SAFELY

Many people like dryfire practice, which is operating the action of the gun with no ammunition. Many believe that dry-firing has benefits for trigger control and general gun handling without the expense or distraction of live ammunition. Dryfiring does carry with it the potential for serious accidents, and even seasoned gun handlers are not immune.

Consciously following these dryfire rules and procedures will greatly reduce the chance for a negligent discharge.

• Set up a specific area in which to dryfire; don't just sit on the couch and haphazardly snap the gun at the television. The area should have a bullet-safe backstop, such as a brick or cement wall or a bookshelf filled with books.

• Take a target and tape it to the backstop; on a bookcase, it would be the side so that a bullet would strike the books on their covers, not their bindings. A case of copier paper from

A quality safe, made of thick steel, is the most secure storage you can get. Photo by Pasquale Murena, courtesy of Cannon Safe

A fireproof safe, bolted to the floor, is the best way to store handguns - and other valuables. Photo courtesy of Liberty Safe

the local office supply store, taped firmly shut, makes an ideal dry fire target that no handgun bullet is likely to penetrate.

• It's a good idea to remove the target immediately after the dryfire session, so that you don't reflexively point a loaded pistol at it and pull the trigger. (Think that's silly? There are lots of cases on record of people doing just that; deaths have occurred.)

• Double check that no ammunition or spare magazines are in the room. Don't allow any ammunition into the room at all.

• Turn off televisions, radios, and cell phones; don't allow any distractions that prevent your full concentration on what you're doing. This prohibition extends to children, spouses, and pets. Do not use alcohol before or during any dryfire practice session.

• Go outside the room and unload your gun (and magazine, if necessary). Leave all the ammunition and any spare magazines or speedloaders outside of the designated dryfire area. Double-check that the gun is unloaded before going into the dryfire area.

• Go into the dryfire area and close the door. Double check

A fast-access safe with a keypad, such as this GunVault, is the best way to store a defensive handgun in a home with children. Bolted to the floor under a bed or in a closet, it allows fast emergency access to authorized users. Photo by Pasquale Murena, courtesy of Cannon Safe

the gun to make sure it's unloaded, then check it again!

• Keeping the gun pointed in a safe direction, engage in your dryfire routine. Remember: your dryfire target should be the safest direction. If it's not, re-think your practice strategy.

• When you're finished, return the gun to its storage area. If it is to be loaded, or you are carrying it, go outside the area to load. Repeat to yourself, "This gun is now loaded. If I pull the trigger, it will fire," several times as the gun is reloaded and stored or holstered. Make sure that your mind has transitioned from pulling the trigger to NOT pulling the trigger!

STORAGE

It's every gun owner's responsibility to make sure that his or her guns do not fall into the wrong hands. Whether it's the curious child who finds a gun his parents thought was completely hidden or the burglar who finds it and uses it to commit a more heinous crime, both can be deterred through proper storage.

IS IT SAFE TO DRY-FIRE MY GUN?

There are a lot of opinions on this subject, ranging from "no!" to "no problem!" The answer lies somewhere in the middle.

Generally, most modern centerfire handguns can be safely dry-fired occasionally without incident. However, it does no harm (and may prevent damage) to use snap caps - dummy rounds which are inserted into the chamber to soften the impact of the firing pin.

Any military surplus handgun of foreign manufacture should ALWAYS be dryfired with snap caps, as should any Colt revolver regardless of vintage. If you plan on regular and extensive dryfire practice, snap caps are cheap insurance for any gun.

Rimfire handguns must always use snap caps when dry firing. Without them, their firing pins can hit the edge of the chamber, eventually peening it so that new rounds cannot be inserted. (There is actually a gunsmith tool, known as a chamber iron, to fix that problem.) Over the years there have been a very few rimfires which claimed to not require this precaution, but it's best to default to using them on any rimfire - just to be sure.

This guy isn't practicing safely. Remove all distractions during dryfire practice: telephone, television - and do not drink before handling any firearm!

A long-shackle padlock can be used to secure and disable both autoloaders and revolvers. (A length of heat-shrink tubing from the electrical aisle can be slipped over the shackle to prevent scratching the gun.)

Remember that there are only two safe places to store a gun: on your person, and in a locked, secured container. If the gun is carried for self protection, keeping it on you - in your custody and control - is the easiest way to prevent unauthorized access. Of course that's not possible all the time, nor is it the solution if you own more than one handgun. In those cases, some sort of secure storage, such as a safe, is the answer.

The ideal storage solution is a fireproof safe that's bolted to the floor. A safe that's not bolted down, no matter how heavy, is easy picking for thieves; you wouldn't believe how easy it is for two people to move a 600-pound safe into a waiting pickup. Bolt the safe down, preferably to a concrete floor. Make sure the safe is well constructed of thick welded plate, and that it has a combination lock. The common stamped steel storage lockers with keyed locks are almost child's play to penetrate, and should be considered no more than toddler deterrents.

Remember that such a safe has multiple advantages; it can

be used to store jewelry, camera equipment, coin collections, and anything else of value.

To keep items inside from rusting, install a dehumidifier rod or use desiccant packages to reduce the humidity. If buying a new fireproof safe, allow the dehumidifier or desiccant to work inside the empty, closed safe for a week before storing any corrosion-prone items; the materials used for the fireproofing

Don't believe that a hidden gun, or one on a high shelf, will be safe from the kids. Children are very good at finding - and accessing - hidden treasure!

material have an affinity for moisture and need time to dry out before use.

It should be self evident, but a safe that's left open is no protection. The safe should be closed and locked at all times, and the combination should not be written on anything in the room. (It's one thing to have it on a piece of paper in a wallet which is always carried, but another to be taped to a drawer in the same room as the safe itself. The former is secure, the latter is not.)

For defensive handguns which need to be kept handy, the best choice may be one of the small fast-access safes. These are sized to hold the gun and perhaps a couple of magazines or speedloaders. These low-profile safes easily fit under the bed or on the floor of a closet, and keep prying hands out while allowing the legitimate user to get to the gun in a hurry. They can also be bolted down, and it's highly recommended to do so

- they're very easy to walk off with otherwise.

One caution: do not buy a safe with a biometric lock, such as those that recognize fingerprints. In personal testing they have proven to be extremely unreliable, particularly if the user's hands are wet, perspiring, or dirty. A better choice is a safe with a keypad that can be rapidly operated by the authorized person who knows the combination.

In the absence of some kind of safe, at least consider locking your handguns so that children can't use them. There are various kinds of devices that can be used to secure a gun, from those that cover the whole firearm to those that lock into the barrel to prevent a round from being chambered. They're not good solutions to a burglary, as they're easily removed with simple tools, but they will keep the children in the house from accidentally firing the gun.

One of the easiest methods to secure a revolver or semi-auto is to simply open the cylinder or slide, and put a padlock through the frame. This prevents the gun from being loaded or even closed, dramatically limiting the opportunity for someone to "play" with the gun. It's cheap, fast, and very effective.

The very worst strategy is to try to hide a gun. Children are remarkably adept at finding things that Mom and Dad don't want them to find, and burglars make their living by doing so. No matter how well hidden you think it is, a gun that's not secured is an accident or crime waiting to happen. If they're not on you, lock 'em up!